THE CHILDREN OF WILLESDEN LANE

A TRUE STORY OF HOPE AND SURVIVAL DURING THE SECOND WORLD WAR

by
Mona Golabek and Lee Cohen

Adapted by Emil Sher

W
FRANKLIN WATTS
LONDON•SYDNEY

This book is dedicated to young readers everywhere. May Lisa Jura's story inspire you to find the music within your heart and the dream you wish to follow.

A Note from Mona Golabek

My mother, Lisa Jura, was my best friend and my teacher. She taught me and my sister, Renée, to play the piano. But those lessons were more than just piano lessons; they were lessons in life. She would always say to me, 'Mona, each piece of music tells a story.'

And in those piano lessons, she told me the story of her life.

I was just a little girl – practising the piano and listening to her tell me about mysterious friends in her childhood and a train ride she took when she was 14 years old to escape the terrible things that were happening in her hometown of Vienna. She told how her music gave her the strength to face so many hard times and an uncertain future.

So one day, I decided to write her story. Together with my co-author, Lee Cohen, I wanted to share that story with all of you. I thought I could inspire readers with a very important message: What do you hold on to in life when facing great challenges?

Since the original publication of the book, the response from young readers has been overwhelming and often profound. 'We connect with Lisa and the violence she faced,' a high school student from Chicago wrote. But the student added that he was inspired by my mother's courage and perseverance. 'If Lisa can do it,' he added, 'I can do it.'

During a school visit in California, one student told me, 'I don't know yet what I want to do with my life, but this book has helped me decide what kind of person I want to be.'

Like my mother, the hero of this book, I hope you discover the courage and direction to be a hero in your own journey and that Lisa's story may help you decide what kind of person you want to be. Know that, despite life's greatest challenges, you can do it too.

Mona Golabek
London, October 2016

Vienna, 1938

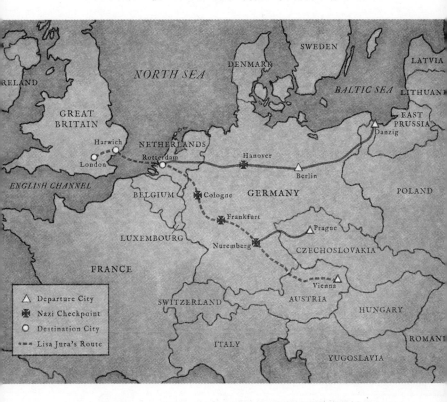

Chapter 1

As she had done every Sunday since her tenth birthday, 14-year-old Lisa Jura boarded the lumbering tram in the heart of the Jewish section of Vienna and crossed the city, heading for Professor Isseles's studio.

She loved the ride.

To go across Vienna was to enter another century – the era of grand palaces and stately ballrooms. As the tram passed Symphony Hall, Lisa closed her eyes, just as she had many times before, and imagined herself sitting perfectly still in front of the grand piano on the stage of the great auditorium. She could hear the opening of Grieg's heroic piano concerto. She straightened her back into the elegant posture her mother had taught her, and when the tension was almost unbearable, she took a breath and began to play.

When she finally opened her eyes, the car

was passing the Ringstrasse, the majestic tree-lined boulevard where the Grand Court Opera House stood. This was the Vienna of Mozart, Beethoven, Schubert, Mahler, and Strauss, the greatest composers of all time. Lisa's mother had filled her head with their stories, and she had made a secret vow to live up to their legacy.

In a booming voice, the driver called out her stop. But today his words were strange and different: 'Meistersinger-Strasse'. Lisa's heart skipped a beat. Why hadn't the driver said, 'Mahler-Strasse'?

As she climbed down into the great plaza, she saw all the street signs had been changed; the Nazis did not approve of such a grand avenue being named after a Jew. She felt her fury grow but forced herself to think about the lesson ahead, knowing that once she was at the piano, the world outside would disappear.

When Lisa reached her destination, she stopped short. A German soldier, tall and emotionless, stood in the doorway of the professor's old stone building.

She had been coming to the professor's

studio for nearly four years, but this was the first time anyone had been standing guard.

He asked coldly, 'What business do you have here?'

'I have a piano lesson,' she replied, trying not to be frightened by the black rifle he held against his grey uniform. 'The professor will be waiting.'

The soldier looked up to the second-floor window. A figure stared down, then motioned that it was all right for the girl to come up. The soldier grudgingly allowed Lisa to pass.

'Come in, Miss Jura,' Professor Isseles said, greeting Lisa with his customary warm handshake. She breathed in the aroma of the white-haired professor's pipe tobacco. For the next hour, she could turn away from all else and be a part of the music she loved.

As usual, there was little small talk. Lisa put the score of Beethoven's *Moonlight Sonata* on the music stand, sat on the worn piano bench, and began to play. The professor sat forward in his chair and followed her progress with his copy of the score.

For most of the hour Lisa played uninterrupted, as the old man sat in silence. She hoped to catch him smiling. After all, she had learned the complicated first movement in only a week and had often heard him say that she was his best student.

Finally, he put down his music and just listened. She looked over and saw a distressed expression on his face. Was she playing that badly?

At the end of the piece, the professor made no comment. He looked at her for a long moment, then finally spoke, looking uncomfortable and ashamed: 'I am sorry, Miss Jura. But I am required to tell you that I cannot continue to teach you.'

Lisa was stunned and unable to move.

'There is a new ordinance,' he said slowly. 'It is now a crime to teach a Jewish child.'

Lisa felt tears rising.

'I am not a brave man,' he said softly. 'I am so sorry.'

Through her tears, she watched the professor pick up a thin gold chain that lay on top of the piano. It held a tiny charm in the shape of a piano.

'You have a remarkable gift, Lisa, never forget that,' he said softly, fastening the gold chain around her neck. 'Perhaps this will help you to remember the music we shared here.'

Lisa stared through her tears at her stoop-shouldered teacher. She was afraid she might never see him again. Gathering her composure, she thanked the professor and collected her things, then turned and fled.

The cold November wind sent a deep shiver through Lisa's slender body as she pulled her coat tight around her and stepped onto the tram. She looked back and saw the professor wave sadly before disappearing from his window.

Why were Germans telling Austrians what they could or couldn't do? It wasn't fair, and why were the Austrians letting them?

The ride was endless, its magic gone. She couldn't wait to get back to Franzensbrückenstrasse, where everyone in the old neighbourhood knew her – the little girl who played the piano. The neighbours knew she had a gift. They could hear her music in the butcher's shop, they could hear it in the bakery – the music drifted everywhere. The street itself seemed to smile when the little girl played. People in the neighbourhood started calling her by that special word: a prodigy.

Music had become Lisa's whole world: an escape from the dark streets; the run-down flats, shops, and markets that were home to Vienna's working-class Jews. And now, the most important escape of all, from the Nazis.

As she neared 13 Franzensbrückenstrasse, Lisa's steps were uncharacteristically slow. She arrived in her living room and dropped her music on the bench with a gesture that alarmed her mother.

'What is it, Liseleh, what's wrong?' Malka took her daughter in her arms and stroked her hair. Lisa cried desperately. Malka guessed what must have happened. 'Is it the professor?'

Lisa nodded.

'Don't worry, I taught you before. I will teach you again.' Lisa tried to smile at her mother's offer, but they both knew that Lisa had long ago surpassed her mother's ability.

Malka went to the cupboard, pulled out the

complete preludes by Chopin, and sat at the piano.

'I'll play the right hand, you play the left,' Malka insisted.

'I can't.'

'Play what is in your heart.'

Lisa sat beside her, playing the four-four rhythm of the marching, repeating chords. When she'd mastered the left hand, she took over from her mother, who watched proudly.

When they finished, Lisa went to her room and lay down, crying as silently as possible into the pillow.

A few minutes later she felt a warm hand on her shoulder, stroking her gently. It was her older sister, Rosie. 'Don't cry, Lisa,' she urged.

Lisa finally rolled over and looked up at the smartly dressed 20-year-old. She was always happy when her older sister made time for her, since Rosie had been spending most of her time these days with her fiancé, Leo.

'Let me show you something I just learned, come on,' Rosie insisted, taking Lisa by the hand.

Lisa stumbled into the bathroom behind her sister and glimpsed her tearstained face in the mirror. Rosie emptied out the contents of a cloth bag and spread the powders and paints on the bathroom dresser.

'I'll show you a new way to do your lips – you'll look just like Marlene Dietrich.'

As she had so many times before, Rosie carefully applied lipstick and eye make-up to Lisa's face.

Without warning, their 12-year-old sister, Sonia, burst through the door.

'What are you two doing in here?'

'Look at Lisa, doesn't she look like a movie star?'

Lisa stared excitedly at her new face in the mirror. She looked five years older! The sound of footsteps approaching stopped them in their tracks.

'Quick! Mama's coming!'

Lisa scrubbed her face with soap and water and Rosie scrambled to hide the cosmetics, as little Sonia looked on and giggled. Rosie put a protective arm around Lisa, and for a moment the sorrow of the professor seemed far away. The three sisters joined hands and emerged to greet their mother.

Chapter 2

'Lisa!' Malka yelled from the kitchen. 'Look out the window for your father.'

Lisa went to the window of their second-story apartment, peering into the cobblestone courtyard.

'Do you see him?'

'No, Mama, not yet.'

Lisa knew what was making her father late: it was that 'gambling' thing her mother got so angry about. He would stay out playing cards with some of the neighbourhood men in the storeroom of Mr Rothbard's butcher shop. Lisa didn't understand a thing about cards, but she knew they made her mother very upset.

Abraham Jura had always called himself 'the best tailor in all Vienna.' Her father was a proud, elegant man who wore starched white shirts with tall collars. His customers had been Jews and gentiles alike. But now Abraham had few sewing jobs, and his longtime customers were turning up with less frequency. Gentiles had been forbidden to use Jewish tailors. A sign on his shop read: *Judisches Geschäft* – 'Jewish Business'.

Sometimes, after she was in bed, Lisa heard raised voices coming from her parents' bedroom. The arguments were about money; that much she could figure out, and it seemed her father was angry at almost everyone these days. Gone were the early-evening dinners and the bear hugs when Papa came home from work to greet his family.

Abraham or no Abraham, Malka lit the Shabbat candles. It was Friday sunset and the Sabbath was beginning. She lit two white tapers in the silver holders that had been her own mother's and turned to her youngest daughter. 'Sonia, why don't you tell us what they mean?'

'One candle is for the Lord, who made the heaven and the earth and rested on the seventh day,' Sonia replied proudly.

'And the second candle, Lisa?'

'We light the second because we observe the Sabbath day and keep it holy.'

17

Malka lit four more candles, one for each of her three daughters and one for her mother, Briendla, in Poland. A warm yellow light filled the room.

Lisa's mother had a tradition of feeding the poor on the night of the Sabbath, and people would line up in the hallway an hour before sunset.

This evening, Malka went into the hallway and said sadly, 'I am afraid we have nothing to share tonight.'

Lisa was stunned. She watched the hungry people shuffle away and saw the sorrow in her mother's eyes.

The girls joined their mother inside and began the meal without their father. When they finished, they watched Malka pull the large mahogany rocking chair to the window. She rocked slowly back and forth, reciting her prayers, eyes focused on the street below.

Lisa and Sonia awoke to loud noises – ominous noises of distant shouting.

Throwing on their robes, they ran to the living room window and saw the sky was red with the flames of burning buildings. Above the shouting came the piercing sound of shattering glass. Brown-shirted soldiers – Nazi Storm Troopers – were running down the block like a band of outlaws, throwing rocks and bricks through windows.

Dozens of neighbours ran out onto the street. Lisa saw Mr Mendelsohn, the pharmacist, racing out of his building, and watched in horror as two elite soldiers – SS men – picked him off the ground, flinging him into the plate-glass window of the pharmacy. She heard his agonised screams, jerked Sonia away from the window, and pulled her little sister back into the bedroom they shared.

'Get under the bed and stay there!' Lisa yelled. She ran into the hallway to search for her mother. Rosie had gone to Leo's.

'Lisa!' She heard the cry on the stairwell and ran down to find her mother holding her father's head in her lap. His face was covered with blood; his clothes were torn.

'It's only a small cut, Lisa, don't worry,' her father said when he saw her terrified expression.

She took one elbow and her mother took

the other, and they walked him slowly upstairs. Malka ignored the blood that stained the sheets and cleaned Abraham's cuts with a warm towel as he lay on the cherrywood bed she prized above all other possessions. Lisa gently picked the shards of glass out of the folds of his clothing.

'I was leaving Rothbard's when I saw a mob. They took turns smashing the windows, the biggest ones first, like it was fun for them. Then they wrote nasty words in paint. They said Juden! Juden Schwein! Kill the Jews. Then one of them threw a bottle with petrol inside a building.'

Lisa was riveted by her father's terrifying words.

'I saw them drag people out of their homes. They took their things and burned them. Children that came into the streets were thrown on the ground. When I was running past the synagogue, they were taking out the Ark and throwing the scrolls and the Torah in the street and setting them on fire!'

He paused to take a breath. 'And there were no sirens. They wanted everything to burn.' It was the night that came to be known as Kristallnacht –

the Night of Broken Glass.

More screams came from the window. They ran over and saw flames shooting out of the house on the corner, and the neighbours were forming a bucket brigade.

'Malka, I need my shoes!'

She said nothing but walked into the bedroom and brought her husband his heavy boots. He laced them up and ran down the stairs to help.

The frightened family stared out the window. They watched the bonfires grow larger as more and more books and possessions were added to the fires.

Suddenly, several Storm Troopers grabbed the men from the bucket brigade and dragged them into the street. Lisa watched in horror as her father was forced to get down on his knees and scrub the dirty pavement. The Storm Troopers yelled, '*Schwein, Juden Schwein!*' and kicked them when they didn't move fast enough.

Malka could no longer bear the shame. She took her two girls by the hand and led them to the bedroom, where they waited in silence for the terrible night to end.

21

Chapter 3

There were curfews now. Jews were not allowed on the streets at night or in movie theatres, concert halls, or most other public places.

Nazi cruelties had continued. Soldiers kept up their attacks on stores and homes, and beatings in the street became a common sight. Storm Troopers broke into homes and arrested many of the men. It was whispered that the men were being taken away to prison camps.

Abraham's tailor shop on the first floor was now closed by government order.

Twelve-year-old Sonia could not understand why all of this was happening. She still went to school, but the Jewish children had been separated from the Gentiles. She was not allowed to talk to any of her friends who weren't Jewish. The day her best friend stopped speaking to her, Sonia came home crying.

'Why, Mama, why?' she sobbed.

'Do you remember the Purim story about Queen Esther and Haman?' Malka asked, holding Sonia.

The girl nodded.

'Haman was the evil adviser to King Ahasuerus very long ago and wanted to kill all the Jews. But the king fell in love with Esther, who was a Jew herself and very beautiful, so he married her and made her the queen. Esther then used her royal power to save all the Jews.'

'I remember,' Sonia said.

'So now,' Malka continued, 'there is an evil man who is just like Haman; his name is Adolf Hitler. He is as evil as Haman, but he can't hurt us if we are brave and act wisely. We must have faith.'

Malka had begged her husband not to go out, but he'd refused. He had gathered his coat and left hurriedly. He had gone out into the streets, pitch black since the smashing of the streetlights.

It was late when he returned.

Lisa strained to hear their conversation.

'We must do something immediately.

The chance may not come again.'

Lisa crept out of bed and stood in the hallway. She heard the words 'Holland' and 'England'.

'They are not letting Jews out of Vienna,' her father continued. 'But they are allowing some trains to take Jewish children. Hundreds have already gone. My cousins Dora and Sid live in London. This could be our only chance.'

'How could we do it even if we wanted?'

'Mr Rothbard said that his wife refuses under any condition to send their son on the train. He will give the son's place to us.'

Malka drew in her breath with surprise and anguish.

'So you are asking me to send my precious daughters away?'

'Malka, he has only one place, for only one child right now. We must send Lisa or Sonia. Rosie is over eighteen, she isn't eligible.'

Abraham's voice was wretchedly unhappy.

'As soon as we are able, we will find a way to send the others.'

'It can't be the time for this. It can't be,'

Malka whispered in disbelief.

Everyone in Vienna had been talking about the Kindertransport – the Children's Train. Far away in England, British citizens, Jews and Christians alike, sensing terrible tragedy, had pressured their government to bring thousands of Jewish children to safety to England – to be placed in homes, farms, hostels. Every Jewish family in Vienna was desperate to get a seat on one of those trains, and now Papa had managed to get one ticket!

Lisa heard her mother's footsteps as she emerged from the kitchen. Malka smiled sadly at her daughter. 'Go to bed now, my darling. Go to bed.'

She kissed her mother's cheek and walked back to her bedroom, where Sonia was sleeping peacefully next to her rag dolls. Lisa stared at her sister and wondered what the decision would be.

The next morning Lisa was reading at the kitchen table when her parents entered the room.

'We have made a decision,' her mother said. 'We are sending you to England. We would like to send all of you, but we are forced to choose only one. You are strong, Liseleh, and you have your music to guide you ... We will send you first. As soon as we can find enough money, we will send your sisters.'

Then Malka began to cry.

Lisa was silent, and although she felt like crying herself, she wouldn't give in to her tears.

'There is an organisation called Bloomsbury House, which has arranged for Jewish children to come to England. It's safer there,' said her father.

'Can't we go together? Can't we wait and go together?'

Abraham looked tenderly at his daughter. 'Sonia will come next, and then Rosie and Leo and your mother and I will join you. Your cousins will take care of you until we get there.'

'Who are these cousins?' Lisa asked.

'My aunt's cousins. I have never met them, but I am told one is also a tailor. A tailor in London.'

Lisa forced herself to conjure up the image of a handsome man in an elegant suit and hat. 'Then I will work for him and send you the money, you'll see.'

The Kindertransport was set to leave the week after Hanukkah. The family lit the menorah each night and said their prayers. No friends came by since Jews were no longer allowed on the streets without a special pass.

Lisa's bag had been packed for several days. She would take only one small suitcase – enough to hold a change of clothes and her good Shabbat dress.

Then, one night, Abraham got the call: Lisa's train would be leaving the following morning.

She awoke before anyone else and walked through the house, determined to remember everything she loved. She stopped at the piano and brushed her fingers in the air above the keys. The copy of *Clair de Lune* was on the piano. Guiltily she rolled it up and put it in her pocket. It was a silly luxury, she thought, since she had so little space, but she couldn't help herself.

Her mother came in from the hall and put on her heavy coat.

'It's time to go.'

The Westbahnhof station was overflowing with people; Lisa had never seen it so crowded. Hundreds of desperate families rubbed shoulder to shoulder in panic and confusion, and pushed belongings of all shapes and sizes toward the waiting train. At the door to each car, Nazi soldiers in long brown coats shouted into megaphones as they inspected suitcases and documents.

When the crowd became too dense, the Jura family stopped for their final goodbyes. It had been decided that Rosie, Sonia, and Abraham would say goodbye first, then Lisa's mother would walk her to the train.

Abraham had been carrying the small suitcase for his daughter. When he stopped and handed it to her, Lisa could only clutch the handle and stand frozen. She felt that if anyone moved from her side, she would fall to pieces like a broken china figurine.

Abraham put his arm around Rosie, easing her toward Lisa, and the two sisters embraced.

'Don't forget to take the window seat so we can see you,' her beautiful older sister shouted above the noise. 'We'll all be together again soon.

Be brave for us.'

Next, Abraham gently pushed his
youngest daughter forward. Lisa kissed her, reached
into her pocket, and slipped the professor's tiny gold
charm around Sonia's neck.

'Close your eyes and picture all of us
together soon … and keep this for me until I see
you again …'

Then Abraham took Lisa in a hug so tight
that neither one could breathe. He was crying,
something she could never remember seeing him
do before.

Finally, Malka took her hand and guided her
through the crowd toward the platform.

Children were lined up, waiting their turn
to board. Some of them were Lisa's age, some older,
some younger, carrying their cherished toys and
dolls. Teary-eyed parents buttoned their coats,
brushed their hair, and laced up untied shoes.

Malka looked at her daughter, who was next
in line, and held her close.

'You must make me a promise.'

'What is it, Mama?'

'You must promise me … that you will hold

on to your music. Please promise me that.'

'How can I?' Lisa sobbed. 'How can I without you?'

She dropped her little suitcase and embraced her mother tightly.

'You can and you will. Remember what I've taught you. Your music will help you through – let it be your best friend, Liseleh. And remember that I love you.'

'Move forward now,' the guard commanded, and waved Lisa up the steep metal stairs. At that moment Malka slipped a little envelope into her daughter's hand. Lisa didn't even have a chance to glance at it. Before she knew it, she was separated from her mother and carried along on to the train car.

Pushed up the steps and swept down the long corridor, Lisa moved quickly to a seat by the window. The glass was covered by the condensation of many fevered breaths, and she furiously wiped a patch clear with the sleeve of her coat. She thought she could see her mother and waved frantically, but she did not know whether her mother could pick her out. She yelled through the glass, 'Mama!' but her voice was lost in a chorus of similar cries.

Finally there was a low clank releasing the brakes. The train began to move, and then everything disappeared into the steam and the smoke.

She looked down for the first time at the envelope she clutched in her hand – the last thing her mother had given her. She tore it open and inside found a photograph of Malka standing straight and proud, taken on the day of Lisa's last recital at school. On the back was written, *Fon diene nicht fergesene Mutter* – 'From the mother who will never forget you.'

The train gathered speed, and the buildings passed in a blur. The snowy fields came into view and the city shrank into the distance.

Chapter 4

Lisa studied the faces of the other children, hoping to see someone from her school, from her neighbourhood, from her synagogue. Yet the train was filled with strangers.

There was a tag around each child's neck. Lisa was number 158. The train stopped several times in the night, and more and more children got on. The newcomers were packed into the aisles and sat wedged on top of their suitcases. There must be 50 of us in this car alone! thought Lisa.

As the children prepared for another departure, there was a loud rapping against one of the windows. An older boy climbed up and lowered it to see what was happening. As the train lurched forward, a wicker laundry basket was thrust into the boy's arms.

He put the basket in the aisle and moved away from it.

Lisa had an odd feeling she could not explain, a certainty about something. She walked up the aisle, stood over the basket, and opened the lid.

Before her lay a beautiful baby, wrapped in a clean blanket and sound asleep. A little angel. She picked it up gently and cradled it. The older girls rushed to Lisa's side while the boys stood back. The car erupted in debate.

'What should we do with it?'

'Does it have a tag?'

'Do you think it's hungry?'

The baby started to cry, and someone panicked. 'If they hear it, we'll all be thrown off.'

Lisa immediately began to hum Brahms' *Lullaby* – the first melody that she could think of.

But the infant continued to cry. Lisa sang desperately to quiet the child, but to no avail.

From up the aisle a 16-year-old girl came and held out her arms. 'I have a little brother at home. Let me try.' The girl took the child expertly and nestled her nose into its flesh. It smiled for a second. The entire car breathed a sigh of relief.

When the infant's crying stopped, she eased

him back into the basket and joined Lisa in scouring the car for juice, milk, and blankets. They took turns rocking and feeding the new baby.

Lisa felt a growing sense of determination. If I can keep strong, she thought, I can make it. I'll make it for Mama and I'll make it for Papa. And soon we will all be together again.

A long, shrill whistle sounded and the train stopped again. The children hid the juice and the blankets and pushed the basket under Lisa's seat. Someone saw a sign out the window.

'It's in Dutch! The sign is in Dutch! We must be at the border!' A hush fell over them.

A stony-faced SS officer made his way down the aisle for a final inspection. He checked names and numbers off a list on his clipboard.

When the guard stopped at Lisa's row, all the children held their breath. Several began nervous conversations to cover the awkward silence that had fallen over the railroad car. The guard opened the lid of the basket and saw the sleeping baby. He stared at it for what seemed an interminable moment, then looked at his list.

'Isn't he sweet?' Lisa asked, interrupting him. And she smiled brilliantly, praying it would distract him. She put every ounce of charm she had into that smile. He turned and looked at her for a long moment, and finally, without uttering a word, moved on, making his way briskly down the aisle. He opened the heavy doors at the end of the car and disappeared into the next carriage.

As the Kindertransport crossed the border into Holland, the lights inside the car came on for the first time, and cheers erupted. Lisa opened the basket and stared at the helpless bundle. 'No one can hurt you now,' she whispered.

It was a bright, moonlit night. Through the window she saw the windmills turning slowly – like in the picture books Papa had shown her.

They arrived at the Hook of Holland, the port on the North Sea. The train stopped, and an excited flock of round-cheeked Dutch women fluttered on board, carrying baskets filled with fat slices of fresh-baked bread and butter and big doughy shortcake biscuits. One lady balanced a tray of steaming mugs of cocoa. The children forgot their manners and charged forward, shouting, 'Me! Me!' as they devoured the treats. The Dutch women smiled at these faces smeared with chocolate.

There was discussion among the women about the baby boy. A serious-looking man with a red armband came up and introduced himself. He was from the Dutch Red Cross.

A group of girls gathered around the baby and watched as he directed a Dutch woman to pick up the infant from its basket. She held it snugly to her chest.

'We will find him a good home here,' said the man.

'How will his parents know where to find him?' Lisa asked.

'I don't know.'

Lisa picked up the wicker hamper and handed it to him. 'Please take the basket,' she begged. 'Maybe someday someone will recognise it. Please keep the basket with him.'

The man smiled sadly. 'Yes, of course,' he said, and took both the baby and the basket with him.

The children emerged shyly from the train compartments and were led through the small station and across the large busy road to the seaport. When they realised there were no Nazi guards to keep them in line, some of the boys began to skip and play and trip the younger children around them.

Lisa ignored the scuffling of the silly boys and looked up at the loud cawing of a seagull above her head. The smell of the sea air, crisp and cool, raised her spirits.

A bearded old seaman in a stiff green peacoat smiled and waved them along the dock toward the ramp. 'Hurry along and up. Next stop is England.'

Halfway up the ramp, Lisa stopped and looked back at the serene Dutch town with its orderly rows of thatched roofs. It didn't look the least bit like Vienna. Where will we end up? she wondered. Will there be an opera house? Will there be a tower like St Stephen's? No time for such thoughts, she told herself, and headed aboard.

She was assigned the top bunk above a whiny 15-year-old who was seasick and proved it by vomiting into her pillow.

Lisa lay awake for what seemed like hours, and looked out of the tiny porthole next to her bunk. The moon had disappeared, and it was impossible to tell anymore where the water ended and the sky began. Eventually, the steady rising and falling of the sea caught up with her and she succumbed to a troubled sleep.

She dreamed of her home on Franzensbrückenstrasse. The family was just sitting down to dinner. Mama was serving her brisket, Papa was at the head of the table, ready to carve. Sonia was there, noisy and impatient, and so was Rosie, stately and beautiful. One chair was empty. 'Where is Lisa?' her father asked. From deep inside her sleep, Lisa tried to respond.

'Here I am,' she cried, but no one heard her; waves of green water drowned out her voice.

By morning they reached the other side of the English Channel. It was grey and cloudy as the single-file line of children walked down the gangplank. They clutched their little suitcases so tightly, one would have thought they carried their hearts inside.

A wiry man with a dark blue coat and a walrus moustache hurried them along. 'There's a train to catch, let's look lively. Hurry along, luvs.'

The single-file line wound through the centre of the tiny English village – looping around the quaint central square and into the train station. It was dawn and no one was up but the milkman. He stared at the eerie sight of more than two hundred children winding through his town. Lisa thought they must have looked like a lost school field trip.

She turned to stare at the vast sea that separated her from her family and all she had ever known.

England, December 1938

Chapter 5

The train rumbled through the English countryside past cows and hayfields, hedgerows and country lanes. Soon the winter pastures gave way to suburbs, and the suburbs gave way to stone buildings, and the journey reached its destination – Liverpool Street station in London.

The two hundred exhausted children were met by a small battalion of well-wishers – nuns, rabbis, Quakers, clergy of every denomination, and Red Cross workers with clipboards. The new arrivals were lined up in the reception hall, sorted, and checked against the lists that had been prepared by the Jewish Refugee Agency at the Bloomsbury House. With a 'Welcome to England, children, we're delighted to have you,' the Red Cross workers moved down the line. Lisa showed her papers and number and was relieved to see her name on the list.

The wait seemed interminable. Lisa watched as half the children departed in a flurry of handshakes and kisses. After what felt like hours, Lisa went up to a Red Cross worker who was handing out cookies. 'Jura, Lisa Jura,' she began, but that was as far as she got. She wanted to say, 'My cousins are coming to get me,' but suddenly couldn't remember the English words she had memorised so carefully.

'Be patient, dear, these things take time. Better get back in line so they can find you.'

The Red Cross worker was leading Lisa back in line when a small man in a worn brown overcoat, holding a photo, came up and spoke to her in Yiddish.

'Lisa Jura? I'm your father's cousin, Sid Danziger.'

Lisa expected that he would hug her, but he held back, bowed his head slightly, and handed her some English treats. He asked about her family and consoled her as she spoke rapidly about the awful state of things in Vienna.

Then he cleared his throat and continued. 'I'm afraid I have some bad news.'

He spoke so quietly, she could hardly hear him above the din.

'My wife just had a baby, so we're leaving the city and, well, we're moving to a one-room flat, you see. There just isn't enough room. We won't be able to take you; we're very sorry.'

Lisa didn't know what to say. These were her relatives, her cousins, the only people that knew her in all of England.

When the man saw the utter terror on her face, he stammered, 'Please don't worry, I personally spoke to the people at Bloomsbury to make sure a good spot is found for you … and the main thing is that you are here in England.'

Lisa couldn't hear all his words. Panic set in again. 'But what about Sonia?' Her voice was frantic. She had fantasised that she could convince them to take her little sister as well.

'We'll do our best to ask our friends. We're not wealthy people, I'm sorry.'

Lisa steeled herself against the disappointment. Mama would have wanted her to be polite. 'Thank you for coming to sign for me,' she managed.

'It's the least I could do,' Sid Danziger replied sadly, and turned and walked away.

Lisa didn't speak during the ride from Liverpool Street station to Bloomsbury House. She was wedged in the huge coach with the dozens and dozens of unclaimed children.

The Bloomsbury House that her father had spoken so much about was a massive stone building in London's West End. Getting off the bus, she saw Englishmen in pin-striped suits and shiny bowler hats walk by, looking just like the pictures she had seen in her schoolbooks.

She climbed the imposing stairs and sat with the others in the hallways. Children were everywhere. The phones were ringing shrilly, and people were shouting in languages she didn't understand.

Names were called, and one by one children went into an office for an interview. Women circulated with trays of sandwiches. Lisa was amused that anyone would put cucumbers on bread and forget the meat, but they tasted good anyway.

'Jura, Lisa Jura,' a voice called, and she was

waved politely into a small office. The tall and balding man behind the desk peered over his glasses and motioned for her to take a seat.

'I'm Alfred Hardesty, nice to meet you.'

Lisa smiled politely.

'How are you feeling?'

'Very well,' she said in her best English pronunciation.

'Glad to hear it. Bloomsbury House is an organisation designed to oversee children like you whom we have helped bring to England during this difficult time, and if you're willing to do some work, you could actually earn some money, in addition to receiving room and board. Does that interest you?'

'Oh, yes, yes.'

'Good. Now what skills do you have? What sorts of things can you do?'

'I play the piano,' Lisa said proudly.

'Well, now, that's lovely, I'm sure you play beautifully, but what do you do that would be more useful? Do you sew?'

'Yes, yes, I sew.'

'Good,' Mr Hardesty said, and checked a little box on the form he was filling out.

46

'I have a sister … in Vienna.'

Mr Hardesty looked at the long line of children before him.

'All in good time, Miss Jura,' he said with a sigh, and stood to escort the insistent young girl gently out of the room.

When Lisa finally arrived at Dovercourt relocation camp in Essex, three hours east of London, she was exhausted and her feet were swollen. The children's holiday camp had been hastily pressed into service to shelter the hundreds of young refugees who didn't yet have homes.

They slept on cots in drafty cabins. Lisa put on her sweater and coat and huddled under the single wool blanket against the damp December weather. She wanted to cry but was too ashamed to have the other girls hear her. Everyone was asleep. She forced herself to concentrate on the Chopin prelude that she and her mother had played together, letting her fingers float through the air over the blankets. Before she could mime the last chord, she was asleep.

The next day, she attended the makeshift English class and looked out the window as columns of cars pulled up to the main administration office. Men and women of all descriptions went in and out of the office, consulting lists and digging through the children's life histories.

Older girls were picked first, since they could work and pay their way. Small children were chosen next by childless couples and taken to homes in the countryside. The rest waited to be sent to hostels and orphanages that were being readied by Quakers, Jewish groups, churches, and kind souls all over England. On the third day of camp, while she was participating in a gas mask training class, a hand landed on her shoulder and she was called to the office.

'Miss Jura?' began a stout English lady in sensible shoes. 'We understand you like to sew, which is excellent, but we'd also like to know if you get along well with younger children.'

'I have a younger sister. I'm looking for someone to help me get her out of Vienna! Can you help? Do you know anyone that—'

'First things first, my dear, let's get you

settled. There's a very important military officer who's turning his mansion into a civil-defence headquarters, and they need some extra help. The lady of the house has a new baby. What do you think, dear?'

Lisa was thrilled at the idea of going to a rich person's home. She'd make them love her right away and then they'd help her.

'I adore babies!'

'It's all settled, then, young lady. Someone will meet you at the station in Brighton tomorrow.'

For the first time since her arrival nearly a month before, Lisa had hope and walked with a springy step back to the cabin. She sat on her bed, pulled out the photo of her mother, and placed it in front of her. Unfolding a sheet of paper she had torn out of her English primer, she began: 'Dear Mama and Papa ...'

She filled the letter with positive thoughts and English phrases she hoped would impress them: 'I am determined not to be thought of as an *auslander* – a foreigner – as long as I'm here. I'll try my best to be a real English girl.' And then she signed it. The well-meaning camp officials hadn't thought about things like stamps, so after dinner, Lisa walked through the double doors to the kitchen and approached a ruddy-faced washer, smiling sweetly.

'If I helped you wash the dishes, would you buy me a stamp for a letter?'

'Of course, young lady. There's a sponge under the sink.'

Lisa grabbed a plate and started scrubbing.

Chapter 6

Brighton, by the sea, was a city renowned for
summer holidays and day trips with family. Winter
was another story.

The train station was hollow and empty
and cold. Lisa was relieved to see a heavyset man in
his twenties holding up a hand-lettered sign with
her name on it. He wore a neatly pressed dark blue
uniform and matching cap.

'I'm Monty,' he said.

He took her small suitcase and led her to an
elegant black car. Driven to her English home by a
chauffeur! If Mama could only see her now.

They drove through the brown countryside,
until the car turned off the main road at a stone
pillar. The sign read: 'Peacock Manor'. At the end
of a long driveway stood a massive country estate
house – three stories tall, with turrets decorating
the left and right corners. It looked every bit like a

castle from her daydreams.

Monty drove the car to the servants' entrance at the back. The cook, three maids, and a butler came out to meet her. 'Welcome to Peacock Manor,' said a lady with a no-nonsense air about her. 'I'm Gladys, this here's Lola, Betsy and Carrie. And this fine man is Mr Piedmont, our butler. You'll meet the rest of us later; come in and take a hot bath and we'll get you some tea.'

Gladys showed Lisa to a small but cosy room in the servants' wing and gave her a starched white maid's uniform. When she was pronounced presentable, she was ushered into the study, where her sponsor, Captain Richmond, and the butler were packing oil paints, easels, and half-finished canvases into cardboard boxes. The captain was a man in his sixties.

'So there you are, missy. Good to have you here. You make sure Gladys treats you nicely!' He winked good-naturedly at the head maid.

'Thank you,' said Lisa.

'My wife looks forward to meeting you; she's off gallivanting in Paris – back next week. Don't mind this mess. I'm giving my painting studio over to the Home Guard; we're certainly not hoping for a war, but just in case … we had best be prepared.'

Lisa was so overwhelmed that she was grateful when Gladys handed her a feather duster and led her up the large staircase into the main hall. 'I can't be bothered explaining everything to you, so just follow along and keep your eyes open.'

Lisa quickly fell into the routine of the castle. She had a keen eye for the dust that gathered in corners, and by the end of the first week Gladys seemed duly impressed.

'You might just work out,' the head maid announced in front of the others at the servants' dinner table.

'And coming from her tough hide, that's a huge compliment,' Monty said with a laugh. He leaned over and planted a kiss on Gladys's cheek. It was a gesture that reminded Lisa suddenly of her father and mother, and she was overwhelmed momentarily with memories; tears sprang to her eyes, so she apologised and excused herself.

That night Lisa wrote another letter to her parents. She described the elegant furnishings and grand surroundings. She realised while writing how happy she was to be settled after weeks of uncertainty and vowed to be useful and cheerful at all times. She arose early and put on the crisp white uniform. By the time the sun came up, she was hard at work, scrubbing floors, fetching coal, and dusting endlessly. She worked with only one purpose – to make the money her parents needed to send Sonia.

Lisa knew the captain's wife had arrived from Paris when she heard the squeal of an infant echoing through the hallways. She was introduced to the 25-year-old lady of the house. Lisa was mesmerised by her elegance.

'I want you to be my lady's maid.'

Lisa's mouth dropped.

'My maid is pregnant and she's leaving. Tomorrow she'll teach you all you need to know.' She waved three fingers quickly in a goodbye gesture, turning back to her cosmetics table.

Every Friday Lisa was paid her salary and she stashed it proudly in a well-fingered envelope in the nightstand where she kept her mother's picture and her copy of *Clair de Lune*. On Saturday, Lisa would accompany Gladys and Monty to the village for supplies. They would pile into an old pickup – with Gladys and Monty in the cab and Lisa in the back.

One Saturday traffic came to a complete standstill. Lisa stuck her head out around the cab of the truck: the road was filled with a long green convoy of British army trucks and tanks, crawling like a centipede. She hadn't seen tanks since Hitler's army had moved into Vienna more than a year ago. 'Are we at war?' she asked breathlessly.

'Just getting ready in case, luv,' Gladys said.

On special evenings, the staff cranked up the old gramophone. The tunes lingered in Lisa's head and she wished she could try them out on a piano. Sometimes she would hum *Clair de Lune* and picture the moonlight glistening off the Danube. If she closed her eyes tight enough she could picture her mother and father, with Sonia and Rosie, walking along its banks.

One day Monty handed her a letter with a German stamp. She was overjoyed to see that the address on the letter was 13 Franzensbrückenstrasse. The letter was short; her mother said simply: 'Make us proud of you; we miss you every day.' Monty put his arm around her when the tears came.

After dinner the staff would gather around the wireless and listen to the BBC broadcast. The news from Europe was upsetting. It had been almost a year since Hitler had taken Austria. In the three months since Lisa had been in England, she had heard nothing to ease her worries.

Lisa was tidying up the new office of the Home Guard (which had taken over the billiards room) when she heard loud voices coming from the captain's study next door.

'I told you this is what it would come to!' a man's voice shouted.

'What were we supposed to do!'

When the voices quieted, Lisa could hear the frightening voice that made her shiver with fear. The voice of the Führer echoed through the manor house: '*Ein Volk, ein Reich, ein Führer!*'

She walked closer to the room where the men were gathered and stood in the hall, listening, terrified by the voice of the man she so hated.

The captain was shouting. 'Can you believe that madman has just marched into Czechoslovakia without a shot being fired?'

He walked into the hall, waving his arms in

disgust, and caught sight of Lisa. 'Aha! Come here, we need you.'

He took her arm gently and led her into the room, where five uniformed men were scattered on chairs in front of the radio.

'What is this maniac saying now?' he asked.

'*Ausrottung, es ist nichts unmöglich!*' came the bone-chilling voice of Hitler.

'Extermination … nothing is impossible,' Lisa translated slowly, growing more upset with each word.

An officer, seeing her distress, exclaimed: 'Have a heart, don't make the poor girl listen to this.'

'All right, dear, that's enough. Thank you,' the captain said.

A young girl shouldn't hear it? Lisa asked herself. I have lived it, I have seen it! She thought of Kristallnacht and saw her father on the ground, humiliated, an image she could not erase from her mind. Suddenly, she was overwhelmed with a desire to be with others like her. Yes, Monty was friendly, Gladys meant well, and the lady was kind, too; she had enough to eat and she was safe; it should be enough, she told herself, but it wasn't.

It was hard to get back to the routine of her job, but Lisa dutifully laid out the mistress's outfits and matched the shoes to the purse and the skirt to the jacket. As always, the lady was very pleased.

'A wonderful choice, Lisa.'

'Thank you, ma'am,' Lisa said. Her heart had been heavy with guilt. She needed to ask the most important question, and she'd been putting it off. 'Madam? May I ask you something?'

'Certainly, what is it?'

'I have a sister in Vienna. She's very sweet and she could work in the kitchen. We very much need someone to sponsor her so she can get on the kinder train, and if there's any—'

The lady looked at her, interrupting. 'How old is she?'

'12.'

The lady frowned.

'She'll be 13 in a week,' Lisa added, exaggerating. 'I'd take care of her on my time off. She'd be no trouble, I promise. She's very well behaved …'

The lady gave her a sad smile.

'I wish I could, Lisa. And you've got nerve for asking. I like that. But unfortunately we aren't able to take on another person ... I'm sorry.'

The words fell heavily on Lisa, and she turned to go.

'Lisa? How old are you?'

'I'll be 15.'

'I wish I were 15 again.' The woman's voice was distant, unhappy. 'When I was 15, I thought the world was my oyster. I thought I was going to make something of my life ...' She looked directly into Lisa's eyes. 'I'm sorry ...'

'Make something of yourself.' The phrase ran through Lisa's mind as she ironed the jackets, pressed the skirts, and polished the shoes. Over and over came the calm voice of her mother – its gentle insistence invading her thoughts. Whom could she look to for guidance if not her mother?

That night she slept fitfully, tossing and turning. In the morning, she was awakened by a rap at the door.

'Are you coming or not, sleepyhead?'

Gladys yelled.

She dressed hurriedly, opened the drawer, and grabbed the envelope that held the money she had saved from her wages, stuffing it into her pocket.

On one weekly trip to town Lisa found the secondhand shop where she had seen a bicycle in the window. She summoned up all her courage and walked in.

'I want to buy this bicycle,' she said, trying as hard as she could to pronounce the 'w' the way the English people did. She saw the curious expression of the shopkeeper and knew her accent was still dreadfully foreign.

'So, you must be that refugee we've heard about. My wife told me we had one of you nearby. And you're looking for a bicycle?'

'Yes ... I have money.'

The man walked up to the bike that Lisa was pointing to and looked at the tag. 'Four pound two shillings. Hmm, seems a bit pricey for what it is. How does two pound sound?' he asked with a wink.

Lisa fished in her envelope and handed a

couple of pound notes to the man. She fought back
a feeling of guilt; this was the money for Sonia! But
she'd make more money soon, she promised herself.

'Can you keep it here until I come to get it?'

'Whenever you need it, it'll be here.'

Chapter 7

Lisa waited until the day after she was paid her small wages, then arose before dawn and packed her things. The sun was coming up when she tiptoed into the kitchen and opened the cupboard. She cut a portion of dried meat, wrapped it in newspaper, and stuffed it in her coat pocket. Using the pencil Gladys kept for the grocery list, she wrote carefully: 'Thank you. I will never forget you but I must go, Lisa Jura.'

She walked the two miles to the village. When the second-hand shop opened, she collected her red bike, tied her small suitcase to the back, and was off. The sun was just breaking through the morning fog as she left the village. The sign read: Brighton – 45 miles.

She was happy; she was going to London! She would go to Bloomsbury House and make them find a place for her in the big city.

As the day wore on and the miles got longer, she was hit by a wave of indecision. Was it terrible to have left a house with caring people who fed and sheltered her? The captain's wife must hate her now; Gladys and Monty must think the worst of refugees. Would she even make it to London?

But she kept pedalling and began to chant aloud: 'I will go to London. I will go to London.'

She entered the outskirts of the city of Brighton at nightfall and followed the signs to the train station. Her muscles were shaking as she got off the bike and limped up to the ticket master's booth.

'The next train to London?' she asked wearily.

'Not till morning, six eighteen, platform four.'

She fished for the required shillings and pence from her pocket, and was handed a ticket.

'Is that your bicycle?'

Lisa nodded.

'You'll have to wait for the afternoon train, then; no bikes allowed on the commuter express.'

Lisa hung her head and wheeled her bicycle

through the station, finally finding the ladies' room, grateful to see a small wooden bench inside. She lay down on it and put her head on her suitcase. She was too tired to dream.

The sound of the flushing toilet woke her up. Two giggling teenage girls in school uniforms were putting on lipstick and laughing. 'Hurry up!' one of them yelled to the other. 'You'll miss the train.'

Lisa hurried, too, grabbing her things and running on to the platform. The train doors were open and inviting. She glanced back at her red bicycle, said goodbye, and boarded.

The compartment was crowded, but she found a seat next to a group of teenage boys with green duffel bags. She supposed they were being called up for the draft as part of the national mobilisation. Their faces were soft and young. She didn't think they stood a chance against the steely-eyed Nazi soldiers she had seen at home, and a dark mood of worry seized her. Lisa tried to distract herself by looking out the window at the lush green countryside, steering her mind on to a more cheerful path of thoughts about the big city ahead of her.

Waterloo station was filled to the brim with travellers. The warm smell from a bakery stall made her stomach ache, and she went and ordered a hot cross bun. She made herself eat slowly so she could enjoy it; it seemed like the most delicious bun on earth.

Following the careful directions of helpful pedestrians, Lisa walked the weary miles to Bloomsbury House.

Chapter 8

Bloomsbury House was still a madhouse of volunteers, arriving children, and file boxes. Lisa walked down the hall and worried what might happen. She'd made her decision. She wouldn't go back. Anything, she told herself, was better than the terrible loneliness of the last six months at the captain's house.

'Lisa Jura? Mr Hardesty will see you now.'

She walked into his office.

'Aha, it's you!' he said as recognition dawned. 'We were worried – the captain told us you'd gone missing.' But instead of the brash young bundle of energy he remembered, before him stood an exhausted girl with uncombed hair and wrinkled clothes.

Mr Hardesty picked up a file with Lisa's picture on the front and several papers clipped to the back.

'Were they treating you badly?'

Lisa reddened in embarrassment. 'No, sir.'

'Were you getting enough to eat?'

'Yes, sir.'

Mr Hardesty let out a large breath, exhaling months of fatigue and frustration.

Lisa forced herself to begin the speech she had rehearsed in her head. 'Excuse me, sir, I came back to London because I want to make something of my life. I don't want to be a servant. I play the piano and I am going to make something of my life. Please, let me stay in London,' she begged.

Mr Hardesty studied her and his expression softened. 'Let me see what I can do, at least temporarily.'

He ran his index finger down a list of telephone numbers, picked up the phone, and dialled.

'I'll get a tongue-lashing, but hopefully it'll be a short one,' he muttered.

Lisa watched as Mr Hardesty wrinkled up his face and began: 'Mrs Cohen? Alfred Hardesty here, Bloomsbury House. We have a bit of an unusual situation here, and I know I promised not to send so much as one more sardine your way, but there's a lovely young lady just needs a place for a month ...'

He held the phone away from his ear and Lisa heard the raised voice of a woman. Cupping his hand over the mouthpiece, Mr Hardesty leaned forward and said, 'I think you two will get along famously.'

Concerned about smoothing Mrs Cohen's ruffled feathers, Mr Hardesty himself escorted Lisa to her new home: the hostel at 243 Willesden Lane. The houses on Willesden Lane were surrounded by neatly manicured lawns. As the taxi slowed, Lisa noticed a building with a cross carved into the stone lintel above the door; three nuns were in the front flower garden, watering the plants. The cab rolled to a stop at the next house.

The two of them got out and headed up the stone walkway. Mr Hardesty knocked, and an imposing middle-aged woman in a dark purple dress opened the door.

'Please come in.' She surveyed Lisa and glanced at the little suitcase. 'Is that all you have?'

'Yes, ma'am.'

'Come in then! Let's not stand here while the house fills up with flies.'

Mr Hardesty picked up Lisa's suitcase and put his arm around her shoulder, easing her through the doorway.

Lisa walked into a dark-panelled foyer, which opened into a pleasant drawing room with two sofas and several groups of chairs and tables. Two well-worn chessboards were arranged neatly on top of a card table. A graceful staircase led upstairs, and a dining room was visible across the foyer. She stepped farther into the parlour and saw the large fireplace and the bay window that looked out on the convent next door. Nestled in the cove by the window was a distinctive shape, covered with a hand-crocheted shawl.

Lisa's heart beat faster; it was a piano!

'We're overcrowded, you know. We can only make room for you temporarily,' Mrs Cohen said, not noticing Lisa's expression of wonder. 'I'll have one of the girls tell you the rules.'

Mrs Cohen's firm stride took her to the base of the stairs. 'Gina Kampf, come down here, please!'

she shouted in a remarkably strong voice.

She has an even heavier German accent than I do, Lisa thought, smiling. She felt comfortable here already.

At the sound of youthful steps thundering down the staircase, Mrs Cohen turned to Mr Hardesty. 'While you're here, Alfred, I have some receipts I'd like to go over with you.'

Before he left the room, Mr Hardesty turned to Lisa and shook her hand. 'Now, please mind Mrs Cohen. I don't want to hear any stories about any more unexpected trips.'

'Hi, I'm Gina!' A pretty, dark-haired girl with vivacious eyes finished bounding down the stairs. 'You must be the new girl.'

'Yes, I'm Lisa Jura.'

'Pleased to meet you!' she said with an exaggerated bow. 'Isn't my English fabulous? Mrs Cohen says I'm the best English speaker in the whole house. Oh, that's the first rule, she says you have to speak English on the first floor at all times. There are millions of rules, but don't worry, I'll go over everything.'

Gina started running back up the stairs.

'Come on, hurry up! I'll show you our room, you'll
be in with me and Ruth and Edith and Ingrid.
I'm so glad you're here; Edith and Ingrid are
really boring.'

Lisa was shown to a bedroom with two bunk beds
and a small army cot wedged against the wall. Gina
pulled open a large drawer and pushed some clothes
to the side.

'Here, you can share this drawer with Edith,
she won't mind.'

The beds were neatly made, and nothing in
the room was out of place.

'Where is everyone?' Lisa asked.

'Everybody's working! We all have jobs.
You'll have to get one, too, you know. I'm only here
because I help Mrs Cohen do the books on Fridays
because my English is so good.'

Gina headed out the door. 'Come on, come
on! I'll show you the washroom. There's only one
for all 17 girls, and we're not allowed to use the
boys' upstairs unless we're dying or something.'

The tour continued. Lisa was shown the
third floor, where the boys slept; met the cook, a

blond Czechoslovakian named Mrs Glazer; and was told too many rules to remember. Curfew was ten, lights out 10.30pm, no food allowed in the bedrooms (for fear of mice), hot bath once a week (to save coal), telephone calls no longer than one minute (egg timer on the table), chores on Saturday, obligatory picnic Sundays (to boost morale).

Gina kept chattering and laughing and gossiping about everything and everyone. Lisa tried to follow it all, but she could hardly keep her eyes open. She heard herself offer a weak thank-you and fell on to the cot for a nap. She'd had a difficult twenty-four hours.

When she awoke, the house was transformed by the commotion of 32 children. German and Yiddish and Czech and English mixed together in the hall. The smell of roasting meat drifted into the room while the sounds of loud footsteps mixed with the screeching of chairs and tables from downstairs.

'Hurry up! You're late, I let you nap as long as I could!' Gina said. 'Mrs Cohen will have our heads if we're late for Shabbes.'

Shabbat! Lisa had forgotten it was Friday. Shabbat! It had been six months without it. Jumping up, she combed her hair, smoothed her skirt the best she could, and ran downstairs.

The 32 children ranged in age from ten to 17 and sat at two long tables in the dining room. Gina had graciously saved the seat next to her for Lisa, who was the last to arrive. A hush fell over the room and all eyes turned to Mrs Cohen, who made a gesture to Mrs Glazer.

The cook then lit the two candles and moved her arms in the circular gesture of the berachah, saying, 'Blessed art Thou, King of the Universe, Who commands us to kindle the Sabbath candles.'

Lisa recited the prayer along with the others, and felt like crying because of the deep feeling it evoked in her. It was the first time someone other than her mother had lit the candles, and she ached for her presence.

Then the challah bread was blessed and passed around the table; each child broke off a piece and ate.

When the prayers were over, the children attacked the platters of food, spooning the chicken and dumplings and string beans on to their plates.

Partway through the meal, Mrs Cohen tapped her fork against her water glass and cleared her throat. 'We have a new girl tonight, Lisa Jura. She is from Vienna. I want all of you to take the time after dinner to introduce yourselves to her courteously.'

When the food was gone, Mrs Cohen again tapped her fork on her wine glass. 'Does anyone have any news they would like to share?'

Everyone quieted down.

'I understand you received a letter today, Paul,' she continued, turning to a blond 16-year-old with wavy hair. 'Is it something you'd like to talk about?'

All eyes turned Paul's way as he said the difficult words. 'My parents have written to say they are no longer in Berlin. Their apartment has been taken away. They are looking for visas to Shanghai. I hope my brother will be coming soon on the train.'

As they all listened, the children thought of

74

their own parents, their own nightmare, their
own hope.

Lisa thought of her parents and wondered if
they would be able to stay in their apartment. She
looked around the table at the others and saw her
own sadness mirrored in their faces. They shared
a terrible anxiety. It was odd, she thought, how
being with others like herself made her fears easier
to endure. Part of the weight of the great loneliness
she had felt since her arrival in England was lifting.
Now, maybe, she could almost bear the long wait
until she could see her mother and father again.

After dinner, Gina took Lisa's arm and sat her next
to her on the sofa, determined to be the arbiter of
all news about 'who was who'.

'See the boys playing chess? The one facing
us is Günter. He's got a crush on me, but I'm still
deciding.'

The front door opened and a 16-year-old
with a leather jacket walked in with a swagger.
Lisa's eyes widened at his handsome arrogance.
Gina waved at him.

'Aaron, come here a minute, meet the new

girl,' said Gina. 'This is Lisa.'

'Hi, I'm Aaron,' the boy replied easily, with a bright white smile.

'Hi,' she said, fascinated by the unshaven stubble on his chin.

'I hope you don't believe anything Gina's telling you, I'm sure none of it's true,' he said, winking, then headed for the kitchen.

'Why is he here so late?' Lisa asked, curious to find out more about him.

'He's the mystery man. Isn't that fabulous?'

The rest of the evening brought a parade of nice faces saying polite words to Lisa. Only one person didn't come forward, a very large boy who had spent the evening writing in a notebook. He was more than six feet tall, and his forearms and biceps were gigantic.

'Who's that?' Lisa asked.

'That's Johnny, otherwise known as "Johnny King Kong",' Gina said, snickering. 'Johnny what?' Lisa asked.

'Didn't you see the movie *King Kong*? King Kong is a big ape just like him!'

'That's not very nice,' Lisa said.

'It's just a nickname, silly.'

But Lisa still thought it was an insult and resolved to be nice to the hulking boy with the serious face. 'What's he writing?'

'How would I know? He doesn't show it to anybody,' Gina answered.

At 10.30pm it was lights-out. Gina was still gossiping when Lisa fell asleep on the bed next to her.

Chapter 9

Gina told Lisa that she was sure the garment factory in the East End, where she worked, needed more girls on the assembly line. Almost all the children of 243 Willesden Lane had jobs, and three-quarters of the salaries of each went to the hostel coffers for room and board.

The garment factory was in the predominantly Jewish part of the Cockney East End and was a three-storey brick building with folding warehouse doors that read Platz & Sons in faded letters. Inside, scores of women bent over long rows of sewing machines. The air was stale and filled with dust.

Seeing her friend's startled expression, Gina laughed. 'You'll get used to it,' she said and brought Lisa over to meet the foreman, Mr Dimble. She kissed her friend goodbye and went to work.

Mr Dimble motioned for her to follow him

into a crowded office. 'Ever use a sewing machine before?' he asked quickly.

'Yes, my father is a tailor.'

'Let's get a little taste of it, then,' he said, and ushered her back on to the floor. 'Mabel, stand up for a second, would you kindly?'

A woman in her forties stood up. Mr Dimble picked up two pieces of navy-blue cloth from the floor, placed them together, and handed the fabric to Lisa.

'Let's give it a try.'

Lisa sat confidently at the machine, lifted the presser foot, inserted the two pieces of cloth, and pushed the foot pedal. She produced a perfectly straight seam.

'You're hired,' Mr Dimble said. 'Come back tomorrow morning and we'll set you up.'

The station at Whitechapel was marked by a large sign: 'London Underground'. She melded into the stream of people passing through the turnstiles, and before she knew it, she was stepping on to a large wooden escalator going down, down, down.

She followed her instructions to Willesden

Green station, got off without a hitch, and headed up Walm Lane. She saw a woman working in the front garden of a brick house. The middle-aged lady wore a plain black dress.

'Good afternoon! I'm a new neighbour from up the block,' Lisa said.

The woman gave a curt nod, then turned back to her vegetables. Lisa shivered and walked on.

The door to the hostel was kept locked from nine to four-thirty, when most of the children were at work. Lisa rang the bell and Mrs Glazer let her in.

'Any luck?' the cook asked in a friendly tone.

'Yes, I start tomorrow,' Lisa replied, and, trying not to sound too desperate, she added, 'Is there any lunch left?'

'Of course, we'll find you something.'

Lisa rested on her bed after eating and pictured the living room downstairs and the treasure it held. It was now or never, she thought. She got up, went downstairs, and walked to the piano, gently pulling back the shawl that covered it.

Looking around guiltily, she lifted the lid. She sat down and stretched her fingers silently over the keys. It had been almost nine months since she had played a piano.

Slowly, she began the opening theme of the Grieg Piano Concerto in A Minor. With a shiver of delight, she attacked the keyboard in earnest.

She felt a strange sensation – as if someone else were playing and she were only a spectator. During a soft, lyrical passage, Lisa's reverie was interrupted by footsteps. She turned to see Paul trying to shut the front door quietly so that she wouldn't be disturbed.

'Please don't stop, it sounds so lovely,' he said, smiling.

Lisa played on as one by one the children arrived home. Without saying a word, they gathered in the living room, on the stairs – anywhere they could hear. Edith slithered to the sideboard and settled in for the concert.

Somewhere into the third, thunderous movement, Mrs Cohen came through the door, carrying a box of groceries; she stopped and stared. Lisa saw her and immediately stopped playing.

'Listen to Lisa!' Edith said proudly to Mrs Cohen.

Mrs Cohen responded with a slight nod and continued on toward the back of the house.

'Oh, play something else, please!' said Günter, coming over to stand by her side.

Thrilled by the attention, Lisa launched into her favourite, *Clair de Lune*, just as Gina came in the door, followed closely by Aaron. When Gina saw her friend at the piano, surrounded by all the boys, she couldn't believe her eyes.

'Gina, come and listen!' Günter said.

In spite of her immediate jealousy, Gina came over and stood transfixed by the music.

'You sound just like Myra Hess,' Aaron said, reverently.

'You've heard about Myra Hess?' Lisa was surprised this handsome boy would know anything about a famous pianist.

'Maybe I'll get tickets next time she plays,' he replied.

Lisa continued playing the Debussy. The room grew hushed, everyone transfixed by the beauty of the music.

Lisa was the star of dinner; she hardly got to touch her food. After the meal, Mrs Cohen said in her formal voice: 'Lisa, would you please follow me to my room.'

Everyone looked up in surprise. Gina looked at Lisa with an expression that said she feared the worst. Lisa followed the large woman to her room in trepidation.

'I see you've studied the piano,' Mrs Cohen said, closing the door behind her.

'Yes, ma'am,' Lisa answered.

'And would you like to practise while you're here?'

Lisa didn't know if this was a trick question, or what kind of answer was expected. She decided to speak from her heart. 'I would very much like to, if you—'

'My son plays the piano,' Mrs Cohen said, interrupting.

Lisa hadn't known there was a son. She didn't have the nerve to ask where he was, fearing he was trapped somewhere by the Nazi nightmare.

'He is in London, in a special school, but he'll be coming here soon,' Mrs Cohen explained.

'You may practise for an hour when you come home from work, then you must let the others use the living room for their purposes. If you like, you may play popular songs for us on Sunday.'

'Thank you, ma'am.'

'Please close the door as you leave,' Mrs Cohen said, and Lisa let herself out.

Chapter 10

Mornings were hurried. Gina and Lisa developed a routine of holding each other's places in line for the bathroom, then dashing in together to spend as much time as possible in front of the mirror before the other girls banged on the door. Gina showed Lisa how to achieve the fashionable pin curls that would best survive the scarves and hairnets required at the factory.

Platz & Sons was organised by floor: women's garments on the third, men's on the second, offices on the first. Lisa was assigned to men's trousers, considered a good place for a beginner. She was surprised by the speed of the work, having been used to her father's meticulous style of double stitching and finished seams. Clearly, the goal at Platz & Sons was quantity, not quality. Lisa was given the machine next to Mrs McRae, a quiet woman who patiently explained the intricacies of the job.

By the end of a day, Lisa's arms ached and her fingers were sore, but she was grateful that the difficult work demanded her total attention – that way she had no time to worry obsessively about her family or whether a sponsor for Sonia had been found.

But of course thoughts of her sister were never far from her mind, and she decided to go to Bloomsbury House later in the week.

The chaos at Bloomsbury House was still in full swing. More children were arriving on the twice-weekly trains – almost 10,000 had come already. Young boys in tweed jackets and ties and girls clutching dolls wandered the hallways. Lisa was again assured that Sonia was on the list, but there was still no word on a sponsor.

Mr Hardesty's secretary handed her a letter that had just arrived from Vienna – the stamp on the front had a picture of Adolf Hitler. Lisa quickly ripped into the envelope.

'Dear Liseleh,' she read in her mother's familiar handwriting, 'I am afraid I have no good news to report, except that, other than your father's arthritis, we are in good health. Sonia is anxious to join you soon, and it is with difficulty that we have patience to await our turn for the train. Rosie and Leo, too, are trying to come up with plans to join you. I pray they succeed. I hope you are practising your music. I will send remembrances from home so you do not forget us. Love, Mama.'

Tears were running down Lisa's cheeks. Forget them! How could she forget them? They were her very soul.

That night, Lisa sat next to Günter and Gina at dinner, and they saw how worried and withdrawn she looked.

'Are you all right?' Günter asked.

'All I can think about is how to help my sister get a sponsor, but I don't know what to do!'

'Where is she?' Günter asked.

'She's still in Vienna. She has a place on the train, but they haven't found a sponsor.'

'You should do what Paul did,' Günter said. 'Paul! Come here!' he shouted down the table. The blond boy hurried over and squeezed in beside them. 'Tell Lisa about your idea.' Günter turned to Lisa and explained, 'Paul's brother is still in Munich.'

'I went through the phone book for people with my same last name, then rang them up.'

'Why?' Lisa asked, not yet understanding.

'I told them I thought they are my relatives! Who knows, maybe they are.'

Lisa's eyes lit up. She would try it immediately. After hurrying through dinner, Günter, Gina, Paul, and Lisa huddled over the heavy phone books of London northwest.

Lisa quickly turned to the Js, Jura. Dragging her finger down the page, she found a Juracek, and then several Justices – there were no Juras in this part of London.

Aaron came in the room, leaned over the phone directory with them, and listened for a moment. 'Try Y instead of J. People change the spelling sometimes.'

She turned quickly to the last page; there was nothing between Young and Yusef.

'Wait! My father's cousin! Danziger! We could look for the cousin's name!'

There were plenty of Danzigers in the phone book, especially in the predominantly Jewish neighbourhood nearby, Golders Green.

'I'll help,' Aaron offered.

'So will I,' said Gina.

'Me too,' Günter chimed in.

'We'll each call four of these numbers tomorrow,' Gina offered.

'We'll call ourselves the Committee for the Resolution of All Ills,' Aaron pronounced.

Aaron put his hand in the middle of the table, and Gina, Paul, Günter, and Lisa put their hands on the top. 'We're the committee, right?'

'The committee we are!'

Lisa received permission from Mrs Cohen to switch her practising to the hour after dinner, so that she could spend time after work canvassing the neighbourhoods. Knocking on doors proved more tiring than she had anticipated. None of the Danzigers said yes.

Lisa had begged the people at work, but they were all as poor as she was. She knocked on shops near the factory, and never thought of giving up –

she'd get Sonia out no matter what.

At the end of yet another unproductive afternoon, Lisa walked up Riffel Road back to the hostel. A voice stopped her.

'Young lady, come here a moment. Please.'

It was the neighbour lady in black, leaning on a large wooden-handled rake.

'I have too many cucumbers and tomatoes this week, would thee take them to Mrs Cohen for me on your way?'

'Of course,' Lisa said politely, surprised at the strange English.

'I'll get thee a bag. Please start under there,' she said, pointing to a dark green plant. Lisa hesitantly lifted the large leaves and was surprised to find half a dozen cucumbers waiting. She snapped them off and piled them on the lawn next to a neat stack of already-picked tomatoes.

The woman still hadn't come back. Lisa waited. Overcome by temptation, she reached for a juicy tomato, and bit in. The woman came out the door just as the warm juice exploded over Lisa's chin and blouse.

'My, my! Look at thee!'

It was just an overripe tomato, but after a day of frustration and exhaustion, and doors shut in her face, Lisa couldn't control herself and burst into tears.

'It's nothing to worry about, I'll get thee a towel.' When the woman returned, Lisa was still crying. The woman handed her a plain handkerchief, and Lisa gradually calmed herself.

'Tell me, what's the matter, dear?' the lady asked with concern.

Lisa didn't say anything right away but finally she found a voice. 'My sister is still in Vienna. Please, please, do you know anyone that could help us be a sponsor?'

The woman's name was Mrs Canfield. She was a Quaker, a member of the Religious Society of Friends. She listened carefully to Lisa, then promised to do all she could. She explained a bit of Quaker philosophy to Lisa, who was in no shape to understand it.

Accepting the handkerchief she was offered as a gift, Lisa backed out the door, carrying the vegetables up the street with hope in her heart.

Two days later, Mr Hardesty called to leave word that a Quaker family in the north of England had agreed to sponsor Sonia and that expedited calls were being made to the Jewish Refugee Agency in Vienna. Sonia would be on the train within the week, and Lisa was delirious with joy.

On Friday 1 September, 1939, Lisa came home early for Shabbat. After the lighting of the candles, Mrs Glazer read aloud from the air raid precautions pamphlet that had been delivered to the hostel that afternoon. The total blackout of London had been ordered. In anticipation of the bombing, bolts of black cloth were to be made into curtains and hung in the windows so that no light would shine through. Gas masks previously stored in the basement were to be placed at the head of each person's bed.

When the sun set that evening, no streetlights came on. Everyone gathered around the radio, which Mrs Cohen had switched on in spite of the fact that it was the Sabbath. The hushed children listened as the BBC reported that one million Nazi soldiers had marched across the border from Germany to Poland in the last 24 hours, with lightning speed, headed for Warsaw. A new word was added to the vocabulary – *Blitzkrieg*.

The next morning, three of the nuns from the convent next door brought boxes filled with tins of food.

'We're cleaning out the larder. We've been ordered to evacuate,' one of them explained.

'Thank you very much, sisters,' Mrs Cohen said.

'We'd like to offer you the use of our basement. The air raid warden says it's the best basement on the block for a bomb shelter.'

Mrs Cohen thanked the sisters profusely, while Lisa helped carry the tins of sardines and meats to Mrs Glazer, who read the labels, checking for non-kosher ingredients.

When she came back to the foyer, the nuns were leaving. One turned back and addressed Lisa. 'We'd like to thank you for the beautiful music. We'll miss it.'

'Thank you,' Lisa said, blushing.

'Miss Jura, will you come with me to my room?' Mrs Cohen said, closing the door.

As Lisa entered Mrs Cohen's inner sanctum, the matron said, 'I understand your sister is to arrive today.'

'Yes, ma'am.'

'Mr Hardesty called me to discuss where to send you. I understand that Mrs Canfield has friends who will take Sonia, but that it might be difficult for them to take you as well. I told him that we would be willing to keep you here, even though we'll only be allowed thirty ration books and you would be our thirty-second person. We'd be willing to tighten our belts a little bit, if you'd like to stay.'

Lisa bowed her head in gratitude and to hide the tears that were being shed all too often. She nodded. 'Thank you very much,' she whispered.

'That's settled, then. Please close the door behind you.'

Lisa went to the door, but Mrs Cohen called her back.

'Wait a moment,' she said, opening the doors of a mahogany dresser and lifting out a stack of sheet music. 'Would you like to borrow this?'

Lisa's eyes widened at the sight. It was Chopin and Schubert and Tchaikovsky! A name was pencilled neatly on the top of each book: 'Hans Cohen.'

'Thank you so much, ma'am,' Lisa cried.

Sonia was due to arrive on the 3:22pm train at Liverpool Street station that afternoon.

The train station was a madhouse. As fate would have it, the children of London were being evacuated that very weekend, and long lines of English toddlers were being organised by their parents and volunteers.

Lisa located the volunteers from Bloomsbury House, and they helped her to find Mr and Mrs Bates from Norwich, who also spoke with the odd-sounding thous and thees. They offered reassuring words about their farm and about their daughter, who was Sonia's age, and together they went to look for the special train coming in on track 16.

The waiting was an agony for Lisa, but finally children began to emerge from the Kindertransport.

Sonia was wearing her heavy maroon coat, even though the weather was warm. When Lisa saw the frail and serious 13-year-old come down the steep steps, she thought she would crumple on the spot from the rush of emotion and relief. Breaking away from the couple, she ran to meet Sonia, grabbing her tightly in her arms, calling her name over and over. 'Sonia, Sonia, you've come, Sonia.'

For a long moment they held each other, and it almost seemed she was home in Vienna again.

Lisa was desperate to make good use of every second of the thirty minutes they had together. The sisters embraced all the way to the first-class café on the second floor of the station, where they were left alone for a private reunion. Grasping her pale sister's hand on top of the white tablecloth, Lisa called the waiter, proudly showing off her English by ordering tea and sandwiches. Sonia politely nibbled at the unfamiliar food, while Lisa opened the package that her sister had brought her from Vienna. Her heart leapt to her throat. Inside was a silver lamé evening purse that had belonged to Malka's grandmother and a book of preludes by Chopin – the one her mother had helped her learn. It seemed like yesterday. She was overwhelmed by emotion.

Opening the letter from her mother, she read: 'Your father and I are so comforted to know that you and Sonia are both at last safe in England, away from the dreadful place that our home has become. We are putting every effort now to find a way to get Rosie out. Take good care of our littlest treasure, Lisa, and know that all our prayers are for the day when we will be reunited.'

Attached to the letter was a photograph of Abraham. She was so grateful to have his picture, for, try as she might, it was harder and harder to remember all the details of her beloved father's face. She stared at the photograph and was shocked to see that his hair was now totally white.

The thirty minutes passed in a heartbeat, and Mr and Mrs Bates returned.

Lisa embraced her sister, trying to reassure the trembling child.

'The minute the bombing is over, you'll come to London with me, I promise.'

Sonia clung to her older sister, too frightened and emotional to respond in words.

'I'm so sorry, but we mustn't be late for the

train,' Mrs Bates said, taking Sonia's hand.

'I promise! Sonia,' Lisa cried reassuringly as the three of them walked away. She watched them disappear, then broke down, tired of being brave beyond her years.

The next morning, at 11.15am, the residents of 243 Willesden Lane put aside their chores and huddled again around the wireless to hear Prime Minister Chamberlain announce formally what everyone had long suspected – that Britain was declaring war on Germany. The rest of the day was spent preparing a bomb shelter in the basement of the convent next door. Everyone pitched in, carrying sandbags and buckets of earth to use in case of fire and stocking the cellar with first-aid supplies. Finally they dragged down their mattresses and linens and set up cosy corners to sleep in.

Lisa looked over at Paul, whose face was drawn and lifeless. He'd been given the news that afternoon that no more transports would be allowed to leave 'greater Germany'. No more sisters and brothers would be coming until the end of the war.

Lisa had been the lucky one – Sonia had arrived on the very last train.

Chapter 11

Britain readied itself for a German attack. Posters were slapped on underground station walls, some showing dashing air force pilots in leather jackets, others showing German soldiers parachuting from the sky – 'How to Recognise the Enemy' they said, and described the German eagle-wing insignias to watch out for. Londoners walked around looking up, convinced the Nazis would be arriving at any moment.

London Zoo brought its animals inside, stuffing boa constrictors and cheetahs into sturdy crates. Anti-aircraft guns were set up in Hyde Park, and in a confusing attempt to throw the enemy off guard, road signs were uprooted throughout the city. Lisa was grateful she already knew her way around.

The assembly line at Platz & Sons was immediately switched over to the full-time production of uniforms, and Lisa's floor now cut and stitched trousers for the Royal Navy.

One day, Mrs McRae, the line manager, seemed less chatty than usual, and at lunch, Lisa overheard the other girls talking about the news.

'Mr McRae has been shipped to France already! Did you hear? Last night, real sudden-like, with no warning at all. For God's sake, don't they have any concern for the missuses?'

'Now, how are they going to keep a secret if we know about it? U-boats'd get 'em 'fore you count to ten.'

'Guess you're right. But they're going to smash them stinkin' Jerries, aren't they? It'll be over before Easter.'

Lisa listened to their conversation but didn't feel enough at ease to join in. They talked so fast with their Cockney accents, it was all she could do to catch half of what they said. She imagined the dark expanse of the English Channel, the grey sky she had seen almost a year ago now, and pictured the men setting out to sea.

She was so grateful they were going; she'd sew a million uniforms for them if that's what was needed!

Now that she'd become a permanent member of the hostel, Lisa was given her own drawer in the bureau, which she filled with her music, the hairnets she needed for the factory, and several new scarves that she had sewn for herself during lunch break, with pieces of cloth she had rescued from boxes of donated clothes.

The hour from six to seven was a favourite time for everyone to gather in the living room and listen to Lisa practise. Since the gift of Mrs Cohen's sheet music, she no longer had to play only the pieces she knew by heart. Part of every session was an adventurous struggle through difficult new pieces, and she longed for her mother's guidance. When the effort to learn something new was too tiring, she would lapse into her favourite, the Grieg Piano Concerto. She played the unforgettable first bars: 'Dum dum, da dum dum', and invariably, someone from the 'committee' would hum the musical response: 'Dum dum dum da dum'. The heroic and tender passages of the Grieg Piano Concerto had worked their way inside everyone's heads, and the musical response to the opening bars had become the call to arms for a committee meeting. Aaron had been the first to do it, and the habit had stuck.

Sometimes Günter would sit on the piano bench to be closer to the beautiful music. As Lisa had got to know Günter, she had come to love his sweet and gentle manner. Sometimes she shared the images of the music that her mother had instilled in her.

'Hear that? That's the sound of the deep blue of the fjords.'

Günter smiled.

'Grieg was from Norway, so I picture this as a summer's night when the sun never sets. Can you see it? Low in the sky.' She played the end of the elegant slow movement, then launched into a staccato dance.

'Ta ta ti da, ta ta ti da,' she hummed along. 'Those are the peasants dancing.'

'Must be exhausting,' Günter said, making her laugh. Promptly at seven, Mrs Glazer announced dinner, and the children rushed to the dining room.

As months went by without the sighting of a single

German bomber, many Britons became convinced it had all been a false alarm. Half of the 800,000 parents with young children who had left for the countryside returned home, and England played a waiting game. Even the 150,000 soldiers of the British Expeditionary Force, who had been sent across the Channel, were waiting, hunkered down in muddy barns in Belgium and France.

Lisa's waiting also continued. When Hanukkah came, a promised visit from Sonia was postponed. In spite of the lull, people said London was still too dangerous.

Chapter 12

Rationing was announced on New Year's Day, 1940. Mrs Cohen sorted through the coupons on the kitchen counter and muttered to Mrs Glazer, 'Four ounces of meat per week per person? Good grief, these are growing boys and girls.'

She took the coupons to the shops on Walm Lane twice a week to pick up the meagre supplies. The bulk of the items were parsnips, potatoes, and flour. The children were assigned turns lugging the heavy bags back home, moaning about the disappearance of sweets and chocolate from their lives. The rations were mere subsistence; Lisa often felt hunger gnawing at her stomach.

One Saturday, when it was Lisa's and Gina's turn, a freak snowstorm transformed the neighbourhood from its customary grey to a brilliant white. After synagogue, the two girls broke off from the rest of the group and went to collect the groceries, fastening the bags on to rickety-wheeled trolleys. The sun was shining for a change, and the two girls skidded home on the icy pavements, laughing their way down Willesden Lane.

Lisa and Gina hurried to finish kitchen duty, carrying the soggy bags of produce to Mrs Glazer in the kitchen just as Mrs Cohen walked in.

'Please come here, Lisa, I want to introduce you to someone.'

Mrs Cohen escorted Lisa to the living room, where a boy in his early teens sat calmly on the couch. He had neatly combed hair and was wearing dark glasses.

'This is my son, Hans. He was hoping you could play something for him.'

'Hello,' Lisa said shyly.

'He will be staying at the hostel with us,' Mrs Cohen added with her usual formality, then turned and left them alone.

'Thank you for the use of your music; I hope you didn't mind,' Lisa said.

'Not a problem. I won't be needing it,' he said with an odd sarcasm. 'Would you play something by Debussy?'

'*Clair de Lune?*' she offered.

'How about *The Girl with the Flaxen Hair?*' he replied.

'I don't know it.'

'There is a copy of the music there.'

'I'm terrible at sight reading.'

'Please?' he asked.

Trapped, Lisa muddled through the first page. When she saw the complicated second page she stopped, too much of a perfectionist to allow herself any more mistakes. 'I'll play you the *Clair de Lune.*' Without waiting for a response, she launched into her favourite piece.

'Mother was right, you play beautifully,' Hans said when it was over.

'Won't you play me something now?' she asked.

There was a long silence before he spoke. 'Yes, I will, if you'll help me to the piano.'

It was only then that she realised Hans was blind. She led him to the piano.

'Please show me middle C.'

She put his thumb on the proper key, then,

hesitantly, he began *The Girl with the Flaxen Hair*, playing with warmth and determination.

Listening to him play, a profound feeling overtook Lisa. How lucky I am, she thought. She had spent so much time thinking about how terrible things were and how worried she felt about her parents and Rosie that she hadn't had time to be grateful – grateful for Sonia's escape, grateful for her own freedom. She knew God had given her a gift, and she vowed to use this gift to its fullest. She would practise and practise; she would fulfill the promise she had made to her mother.

Chapter 13

Hans spent his days in the living room, reading books in braille and listening to the radio. His only respite was Lisa's practice session. Each evening when she returned from work, he happily joined her at the piano bench, tapping his cane to the rhythm of her Czerny exercises and offering praise and suggestions with each new piece she'd tackle.

After each session, he returned again to the radio. The recent news had been grim. The Nazis had landed in Norway, invaded the Netherlands, and entered Belgium, Luxembourg, and the north of France.

On the third Sunday in May, Hans spread the word that there would be an important broadcast that evening, the first speech by the new prime minister. Almost all of the thirty residents crowded into the living room as Hans turned up the volume.

Winston Churchill's voice was powerful and magnetic, and they leaned forward to hear every word. 'I speak to you for the first time as prime minister in a solemn hour for the life of our country ... A tremendous battle is raging in France and Flanders. The Germans have broken though the French defences north of the Maginot Line, and strong columns of their armoured vehicles are ravaging the open country ... It would be foolish to disguise the gravity of the hour. It would be still more foolish to lose heart and courage ... for myself I have invincible confidence in the French army and its leaders ...'

When Lisa went to bed that night, she was trembling with fear. She pulled out the pictures of her mother and her father and held them close to her as she fell asleep.

Two weeks later, Lisa received two letters. One was from Sonia. 'I have enough to eat and am learning to speak English, but I miss you very much and ...'

The second letter was very disturbing. It was her own letter to her parents in Vienna, addressed to 13 Franzensbrückenstrasse, which had been sent back stamped 'Undeliverable'.

Lisa called a 'committee' meeting, in despair. Günter, Gina, Paul, Aaron, and Lisa gathered around the dining table and shared their worries – none of them had received any recent news of their parents. They agreed to meet at Bloomsbury House the next day after work.

The beleaguered old building was familiar by now. The Jewish Refugee Agency offices inside were still overcrowded, no longer with lost children, but with desperate relatives searching for news.

The five teenagers convinced the volunteer secretary that they had to see Mr Hardesty himself.

'And how is Willesden Lane?' he asked as they were ushered into his office.

'Mr Hardesty, we do not have one word from our parents,' Lisa said. 'No one is giving us any information.'

Lisa handed Mr Hardesty a handwritten list of the names of all their parents. 'Please, can you find out where they are?'

He took the list of names and read it, then leaned back in his chair. 'We know very little. The Red Cross is trying to find out all they can. All we know is that many Jews are being sent to relocation camps, and that is why you are not receiving letters.'

'Camps?' Gina asked.

'Relocation camps, we know very little about them. I'm sorry. Now, if there are questions about England, I'd be—'

Aaron stood up rudely and headed for the door. The rest followed, but Lisa stayed for a second.

'Thank you, Mr Hardesty,' she said.

When Lisa and Gina went to work the next day, the tabloid headlines reported the worst: 'Paris falls to the Nazis – De Gaulle flees to England'. Lisa took Gina's hand and began to walk faster.

'We can make it, we can make it,' they chanted, pushing the fear away.

At Platz & Sons, Lisa took her place at the machine and began another tiring day. She noticed that Mrs McRae in front of her was wearing a black armband. At lunch her worst suspicions were confirmed.

'Did you hear?'

'Mr McRae. Killed in Belgium, he was, never made it to the beach for the boat lift.'

'Just found out yesterday, she did. Can you believe she's come to work today?'

'That's what I'd do, if it were me.'

The workers ate quickly; their lunch break had been cut to 15 minutes. Lisa went back to work filled with awe for the British people, who didn't seem to cry, who sacrificed everything. She watched Mrs McRae's hands tremble as the woman sewed uniform after uniform.

'I'm very sorry to hear what has happened,' Lisa said softly. Mrs McRae took her hand and pressed it warmly, saying nothing, then lifted another trouser leg on to her machine.

A badge pinned to Mrs McRae's lapel read: Support Our Men in Arms.

The fall of France left Britain alone to face Hitler, and the British steeled themselves for an expected invasion.

There was a growing sense of paranoia about enemy aliens in their midst. Women who were too blond were suddenly 'suspect'. A poster showing a sleek, sophisticated blond socialite surrounded by doting soldiers admonished: 'Keep mum, she's not so dumb.'

People were looking everywhere for spies. Workers of German and Austrian ancestry were laid off, and 50,000 immigrants – 'aliens', they called them – were rounded up and put behind barbed wire in racetracks, at factories, and on distant islands, such as the Isle of Man.

It was long after lights-out in the hostel when the whistle of the Grieg Piano Concerto in A Minor sounded insistently from the hallway outside Lisa's bedroom. She leapt out of bed and shook Gina. They dressed and rushed downstairs to the dining room, where Aaron, Hans and Paul stood in their pyjamas, holding a candle.

'Günter isn't back,' Aaron said, worried.

It was only midnight; some of the others had been known to sneak in that late, but Günter? He was never late.

'What should we do?' asked Paul.

'You should wake your mother,' Paul said to Hans.

'Why me? I'm already blind. I don't want to lose my ears, too.' They had all come to accept Hans's sarcastic humour.

The boys looked at Lisa, the meaning clear: she was the favourite, so it would fall to her to wake Mrs Cohen.

She knocked gently on the door, but there was no response, so she had to rap as loudly as she could. 'What is it!' came the angry response.

'Günter hasn't come home.'

'Who?'

'Günter's missing!' Lisa yelled through the door.

Mrs Cohen appeared a minute later in the hallway, her long grey-brown hair loose on her shoulders, not in its normal place on top of her head. She grabbed the telephone in the alcove and ran her finger down a list of telephone numbers on the wall.

'Is this the police station? This is Mrs Cohen from the refugee hostel on Willesden Lane. I'm missing one of my charges.'

Lisa watched as Mrs Cohen's face darkened.

'Enemy alien! Is this a joke? He's a young

boy,' she shouted into the phone.

'I know he's 16, I know he's German …
What do you mean he'll be interned! He's Jewish!'

Mrs Cohen slammed down the phone and
opened a thick handwritten book listing the names
and addresses of each resident's employer.
Finding the number of Mr Steinberg, the man
Günter worked for, she dialled and explained the
situation, then nodded in gratitude. 'Thank you
so much.'

'Mr Steinberg is English,' she explained to
the concerned teenagers. 'He'll go right away to the
police station and vouch for Günter's loyalty. Now
go to bed,' Mrs Cohen said.

They didn't. They lit more candles and sat
around the dining room table and waited.

'Sixteen? Did Günter have a birthday?'
asked Paul.

'Last week. He didn't tell anybody but me,'
Gina said.

Aaron wandered into the dark living room
and came back with the chessboard. He set up the
pieces, and he and Hans played several games. The
blind boy beat him almost every time.

At the back of the house Johnny was sitting on a milk crate, writing in his notebook by candlelight.

'Johnny! What are you doing?' Lisa asked.

'When I can't sleep, I write,' he said nervously.

'May I see?' Lisa asked, leaning over to see, but Johnny put his huge hands over the page to cover it.

'Oh, no, no. It's not any good,' he insisted.

'Maybe you'll show me some other time,' Lisa said, smiling, and headed out into the back garden.

At two in the morning, Hans and Aaron were still playing an endless endgame, chasing each other's king back and forth across the board. Lisa was bored silly.

'Hans,' she said, 'do you mind if I ask you something personal?' She tried to sugarcoat the question she had been wondering about for so long. 'Have you always been blind?'

He felt where Aaron had left his pawn, then let out a sigh, trying as hard as he could to sound flip. 'No, God gave me this as his special present last year.'

'Last year?'

'A mob at school beat me up the day after Kristallnacht. The actual diagnosis was that a chair leg hit my optic nerve. But not to worry, the rabbi said it was a gift.' His voice dripped with sarcasm.

Lisa was stunned. 'Why did he say that?'

'He said it was a gift because otherwise my mother would never have taken me out of Berlin. We'd still be there. She would never have left; she never thought it would happen to her.' He paused for a breath, then went on. 'You want to know a secret? She's never been to a synagogue.'

The room was silent for a moment. Then Hans put his hands on the chessboard again and made his move.

'Checkmate.'

At 3am the committee adjourned and went to bed.

When Günter finally came in late the following evening, he was surrounded by his friends. 'Tell us what happened!' they said in unison.

Günter had been on the double-decker bus coming back from work. His seatmate looked over, saw Günter writing a letter in German, and called

118

the police to arrest him as a spy. Günter explained that he was writing a birthday card to the daughter of his employer and that he was Jewish; why would he be a spy? But he had a German accent and an alien registration card and was taken to the station.

Jewish or not, aliens over 16 were being interned. Luckily, Mr Steinberg showed up in time and signed an affidavit stating that Günter's work at his factory was 'critical to the war effort, and without him, the assembly line would shut down.'

Lisa turned to Paul and Aaron with a worried look. 'How old are you?'

'Fifteen,' they replied in unison.

'But still, you better be careful.'

When Lisa and Gina were getting up from the table, Johnny came and slipped Lisa a piece of paper, then left silently.

Lisa opened the envelope and read: 'Please do not show this to anyone else.' She turned away from Gina and unfolded a poem.

Always I see the faces

The faces at the station

The faces at the station

Are dimming before my eyes …

Always I hear the voices

The voices that are calling

That are calling out to me

But yet I cannot answer.

My mother, my father,

My sister, my brother

They are here now

Always

My heart is with them.

She looked up and saw Johnny staring at her from across the room. She was very moved by the simple words. Somehow his poem struck a chord in her heart in a way that was usually reserved for music alone. She winked at him and he smiled back, raising his pen as a salute.

She folded the paper neatly and put it in her pocket, safe from prying eyes.

Chapter 14

In the summer of 1940, the war came to the skies over Great Britain. Newspapers were awash in headlines of dogfights between the German Luftwaffe and the British Royal Air Force. The coastline of southern England was hit first as the Germans went after airfields and radar installations.

On 7 September the London Blitz had begun. Over the next forty-eight hours, the children of Willesden Lane went back and forth, day and night, into the shelter. When the weekend was over, two thousand tons of bombs had been dropped on to the docks and the industrial area of the Cockney heart of London – right in the neighbourhood of Platz & Sons.

As the weeks went on, wave after wave of bombs continued their assault on the East End. In one terrible night alone there were a thousand fires. Workers began grumbling that their neighbourhood was taking the beating for the whole country. Lisa and Gina and the other workers started leaving early so that they could make the trip home before the sirens went off again. Lisa would run into the hostel and grab as many precious minutes on the piano as she could before another siren would blast.

One night, after an all-clear, they picked up leaflets that had fallen from the sky. 'A Last Appeal to Reason' one read. The text was by Adolf Hitler and urged the English to give up before they were obliterated. Everyone laughed, but Lisa couldn't help wondering if the joke was on them.

When Britain gradually got the upper hand in the daytime, downing one Nazi bomber after another, the Germans switched and bombed only at night. They had learned a costly lesson: this would not be the quick victory they had expected – for the first time since 1936, they couldn't roll in and over a country in a matter of weeks.

In a fit of patriotic fervour, Johnny announced that he had signed up for the 'rescue squad.' He showed off his metal helmet proudly, its large letter R painted across it.

'You're only 15, John,' Mrs Cohen said,

chastising him.

'I wasn't asked my age, ma'am,' he replied. 'Only my weight,' he added, provoking giggles from the group. Johnny was enormously strong, and God knew the rescue squad could use him. Lisa went up and gave him a patriotic kiss.

One night, huddled in the shelter, Lisa tried to figure out how she, too, could help the war effort. What could she do? She wasn't strong like Johnny. All she could do was play music. Suddenly it hit her; she could help raise morale by organising a 'musicale', a little concert of classical music and popular songs, and invite refugees from another hostel. The matron gave her approval; everyone was very excited. It gave them a sense of patriotic purpose.

Lisa asked for suggestions from Mrs McRae about popular songs, and people at work donated sheet music. Lisa's favourite was *Oh, Soldier! Who's Your Lady Love?*

Hans agreed to play his favourite, *Be Like the Kettle and Sing*, which he had memorised from the BBC broadcasts.

Gina wanted to help. 'Let me sing the words.'

'You can't sing,' Lisa said without thinking.

'I can too. You just don't want anyone else to get any attention!'

Gina pouted for several days, until, realising the programme wouldn't be the same without her friend's enthusiasm, Lisa grovelled and begged her to sing. They all stayed at the piano, practising until the last seconds of the now daily air raid blast, then had to be dragged by the matron into the shelter, still singing as loudly as they could.

The musicale was scheduled for New Year's Day, 1941. Mrs Glazer had been hoarding butter so that she could make mincemeat pies, and the other hostel forwarded two weeks' ration coupons for sugar. Gina was in good voice, only half joking that she was considering a singing career, and Günter scrounged up a pair of castanets. Edith borrowed a neighbour's oboe and learned the five most relevant notes, while Johnny beat the time on his metal helmet.

A week's lull in the bombing raised everyone's spirits and enabled the entertainers to put the finishing touches on their music programme. But on 29 December, the air raid siren sounded once again in the middle of evening practice. Everyone moaned and grabbed their books and the chessboard and headed underneath the ground. Everyone but Lisa.

She was fed up with the horrible shelter. She needed to keep practising! She played feverishly, her chords her only ammunition. She played with such intensity that she couldn't hear that the bombs were coming ever closer.

Suddenly there was a deafening crash, and the force of the bomb's concussion threw Lisa from the piano and smashed her against the living room wall. The glass of the bay window shattered and sent splinters showering across the room.

Lisa lay on the floor, wondering if she was dead. She looked at her hands first; the fingers moved, and so did the arms! She did a muscle-by-muscle inventory and discovered that everything worked. She was covered in dust and splinters but could discover no blood, so she stood up slowly. Instead of being terrified, she felt suddenly calm. These bombs can't hurt me! she told herself. She was fine; the piano was fine! The door flew open and Aaron and Günter ran in.

'Lisa! Are you all right?' they yelled
in unison.

'Just fine, you can tell Mr Hitler I'm
just fine!'

'I'll tell Mr Hitler that you're crazy! Now
let's go!' Aaron shouted angrily. She had never seen
him so upset.

Another wave of airplanes was approaching;
Aaron and Günter each seized one of her arms,
lifting her up and over the glass and back to
the shelter.

Once underground, Mrs Cohen grabbed
Lisa, clasping her to her chest in relief. Releasing
her, Mrs Cohen scanned her charge from head to
toe, making sure she was intact. Satisfied that Lisa
was unharmed, she railed: 'We are at war, young
lady! It is not the time to take foolish risks. I had to
send two boys to find you. You could have all been
killed! Never, never do that again!'

Lisa apologised, too overcome to try to
explain herself, and set about comforting the
younger children. The raid lasted another six
long hours. It was dawn when the neighbourhood

emerged from its shelters. The smell of smoke hung in the air with the dust and the fog. Four houses on the block, including the hostel, had been hit, and rescue crews were looking for the residents of 239. Their back garden had taken a direct hit and the shelter was covered with bricks and debris. Firemen were frantically digging them out. Everyone held their breath until finally the dusty man and wife appeared at the entrance and waved.

Willesden Lane cheered. They'd been lucky.

Lisa and Gina stood on the pavement and watched the firemen inspect the hostel. A hole was ripped through the roof, and windows were completely blown out. When the firemen came out and gave the thumbs-up, Lisa joined a dozen others in rushing back into the building.

'Be careful, there's broken glass all around!' Mrs Cohen yelled, but nothing she said could stop them.

Lisa had only one thought: Where were the photos of her mother and her father? She ran into her bedroom. Yanking open the drawer of the bureau, she pulled out their pictures, still intact, not even damp. She read for the millionth time: *Fon diene nicht fergesene Mutter* – 'From the mother who will never forget you'.

'I'm safe, Mama,' she whispered, hoping to communicate across the distance to wherever her mother was. She wished so much she had news of her ... Where could she be?

Mrs Cohen pulled her from her thoughts by tugging gently on her sleeve. 'Please hurry, Lisa, pack your things, we have to go.'

The 32 children were led to the community shelter to spend the night. They were officially homeless once again.

Chapter 15

No one knew exactly when the hostel would be habitable again. After the broken glass had been cleared from the front room, the residents were called back to the house for a brief meeting. They were told to sit in the living room. Günter, Aaron, and Johnny pushed the piano away from the cold air blowing through broken windows.

Mrs Cohen addressed the disheartened assembly. 'Quiet, please, for just a moment!' When the noise died down, she continued. 'Mrs Glazer and I have spent today contacting our neighbours and asking them if they could host you until our home is liveable again. We have done our best to find you all homes as close by Willesden Lane as possible. Unfortunately, some of you will be placed outside of London temporarily ...'

A murmur of disquiet went through the group. 'Please be patient, and bear with me!' The matron looked genuinely distraught.

'I know how important it is to all of you to remain in contact with each other; we've become a family. So you have my promise that I will do everything in my power to get our hostel repaired as soon as possible. Please wait until your name is called.'

Lisa sat still for the next hour and watched her housemates and friends leave one by one. First Gina, then Günter, then Aaron, her spirits sinking lower and lower as her friends left.

'Lisa Jura,' Mrs Cohen said finally, and the Quaker lady in black stepped into the foyer. Lisa looked up at her, surprised. This woman had done so much for her already!

'Hello, dear Lisa,' said Mrs Canfield. 'Will thou forgive me for being so late? I wanted to get here early, but I was held up at a meeting.' She took Lisa's hand and helped her gather her belongings. Together they walked down the lane to Riffel Road.

Lisa paused shyly in front of her new home.

'Come in, please. Consider this house thine own,' said Mrs Canfield, as Lisa stepped into the foyer. The furnishings were very simple – and there was no piano.

'I'm sure it is difficult being separated from your friends, but I will try to make thee a home nonetheless,' Mrs Canfield said kindly, leading her up the stairs to a tiny bedroom. On the bureau was a framed photograph of a thoughtful-looking young man in a military uniform.

'That's my son, John. He's somewhere in Africa. He would be happy to know his room is being put to good use.'

'He's very handsome,' said Lisa, trying to make conversation.

'He's a medic,' Mrs Canfield said, looking at the photo lovingly. 'We don't believe in fighting, of course, but he's doing his part to help his country. I'm very proud of him.'

One night as Lisa lay in bed during a lull in the bombing, she heard a familiar whistling at her bedroom window. At first she thought she must be dreaming – but there it was again, the unmistakable melody of the Grieg Piano Concerto. She jumped up and saw Aaron at the window. She rapped on the glass as an answer, then tiptoed through the house and opened the front door.

'Aaron!' she said excitedly.

'Hello, Miss Jura … lovely evening, isn't it? Care for a stroll?' he asked.

'I'll get my coat!' She ran back and bundled herself up, paying careful attention in the mirror to the twist of her muffler.

As they walked down Riffel Road, Aaron filled Lisa in on where he was living and how awful it was. His host family was even more strict than Mrs Cohen. 'Never mind all that … I want you to meet me tomorrow for lunch. I have a surprise for you.'

'I only get fifteen minutes for lunch. You know that,' she chastised him.

'Trafalgar Square, at noon,' he said commandingly.

In a battle of wills, Lisa was usually the winner. 'I refuse to come unless you tell me what it is.'

Aaron stopped for a second to prolong the suspense, then relented. 'Myra Hess.'

Lisa jumped for joy, throwing her arms around him.

'Mr Dimble, I'm sorry, but I have to go somewhere at lunch today. I need an extra hour, please.'

She hated to lie to Mr Dimble, but that's the way it had to be.

'I have to renew my alien registration card,' she fibbed, hoping he wouldn't know much about it. 'I'll stay late and make up the time.'

'Does it have to be today? Fridays are much easier,' he said.

Lisa thought fast. 'Tomorrow's my birthday, I have to do it before tomorrow.'

'If it has to be, all right. I'll have someone cover your spot.'

She ran up to the third floor to find Gina in the lunchroom and asked her to keep her secret. Then she flew out the door and into the tube station.

At Trafalgar Square she saw Aaron leaning on the huge bronze of the lion's ankle.

'Ready?'

'Ready!'

She grabbed his hand, running across the street and into the imposing National Gallery. A mammoth nine-foot grand piano was at the end of the gallery and hundreds of chairs were filling up fast with music lovers. She pulled Aaron by the hand and found the seat with the best visibility.

A diminutive woman with short dark hair entered to a thunderous standing ovation and stood by the piano bench. 'This performance is dedicated to the brave men and women who are serving our beloved country – Britain,' she announced.

A shiver of pure exhilaration went through Lisa as the opening hush fell over the audience and the concert began.

The bell-like tone of the Steinway grand enveloped the large hall and filled Lisa's heart. She allowed her mind to wander to the fantasy that had so often filled her in Vienna, of playing in front of a grand audience herself in a huge concert hall; for an instant it seemed almost real. Lisa sneaked a look at Aaron and noticed there were tears in his eyes.

She lived a thousand dreams in the next forty minutes. Lisa hated when the beautiful notes slipped away and the concert ended. There was so much she wanted to say to Aaron but she was needed back at the factory. She gave him a hurried thank you hug and ran for the bus.

At lunch the next day she was embarrassed to hear Mrs McRae and the other workers sing her a verse from 'Happy Birthday.' Gina began to laugh at Lisa's dismay but stopped when Lisa shot her a warning look. After blowing out the single candle on top of the tiny cupcake, Lisa split the sweet dessert with her as a payoff for her silence.

'I have some news,' Gina said. 'I'm not going to work here anymore.'

'What do you mean? Why not?' Lisa asked, surprised and alarmed.

'The lady where I'm staying wants me to help take care of her new baby.'

'Oh, no! How far away is it?' Lisa asked.

'Forty minutes by train. Not so bad, I guess.'

Lisa felt suddenly abandoned.

'I won't just be a servant, though,' Gina said to cheer things up. 'The lady says I can go to school in the morning! Isn't that wonderful?'

'Yes, it is,' said Lisa, trying to hide her sadness as the buzz of the lunchroom disappeared into the inner silence of another loss.

The whistle of the Grieg again sounded at Lisa's

window that evening. Having hoped it would come again soon, she had laid out her shoes, her coat, and a muffler just in case. She tiptoed out the front door, leaving it slightly ajar.

She and Aaron strolled through the streets, darkened by the blackout. It was blessedly quiet, though every few minutes a search beam would sweep the sky for enemy aircraft. They strolled slowly toward no destination in particular.

Aaron was as sweet and gentle as he had been the day before. She couldn't figure out what would make his moods so different from one day to the next. Sometimes he'd be sarcastic and bitter, then gracious and sentimental, as he was now.

'Any news of the committee?' Aaron asked.

'Gina's got a new job as a nanny.'

'I wonder how long that'll last?' He laughed. 'Oh, did you hear about Paul?'

'No, is he all right?'

'They picked him up the day after he turned sixteen. He's on the Isle of Man.'

'That's terrible,' Lisa said. 'How could they? It's so stupid.'

'It's so British.'

'That's mean.'

'But don't worry,' Aaron said. 'Günter got a letter from him. He says he's fine and that the food is better than it was at the hostel. Says there are lots of Nazis and spies, but they don't say much or they'll get beaten up. In six months they're going to let him enlist in the army.'

They kept walking and passed the entrance to the tube station at Willesden Green.

'Aaron, I want to ask you something personal. Please don't be angry,' Lisa began.

Aaron didn't say anything, so Lisa continued.

'What were you crying about yesterday at the concert?' She had been reliving this moment for the last two days.

Aaron was silent for a moment.

'I was remembering the chamber music at our house,' he said finally.

'You had chamber music at your house?' she said, surprised.

'When I was younger I used to fight with my mother about having to go downstairs and listen – all I wanted to do was stay in my room and build

137

bridges, like my father did. I had hundreds of metal strips and screws and bolts that my father had made for me ...' His voice drifted off for a moment. 'Sunday nights, though, they made me listen to chamber music in the salon. You would have loved it.'

'But why were you crying?' she asked gently.

'It's what happened when the chamber music stopped. My father was very influential in Mannheim, you see, just like his father and his father's father. He had designed the major new bridge over the Rhine. The members of the philharmonic came to the house, so did the mayor. I mean, they used to come before they were told not to – by the Nazis.' Aaron disappeared for a while into the memory of his story.

'And then?' Lisa asked, prodding gently.

'Then nobody came to the house anymore. And they closed my father's office. One Sunday night, he dressed up again in his black tie, opened the front door and waited for the guests to arrive. My mother was crying as she watched him waiting and waiting. Of course, nobody came.'

Lisa waited as Aaron exhaled a huge sigh.

'Then he walked out the door …'

Lisa waited for Aaron to go on, but he didn't. 'Then what happened?'

'They found him floating in the river … near the bridge he had built.'

Lisa started to cry and he took her hand. They walked quietly through the streets. At the corner, in the dark under the streetlight, he put his arm around her and kissed her. She felt her heart beginning to give way.

Chapter 16

In the spring of 1941 the crocuses came up in the front garden of 243 Willesden Lane and were a welcome mat of purple flowers for the reopening of the hostel. Repairs had been expedited at the insistence of Mrs Cohen, who wanted her charges to be reunited as soon as possible. They had been away for several months. On the day of the move, Mrs Canfield escorted Lisa around the corner to the hostel, embracing her as they said goodbye.

'I promise I'll come and visit,' Lisa said.

'That would make me very happy. I hope thou knowest how comforting it was to have thee – it helped me so with my worries about John so far away. My house will always be thy house.'

Mrs Cohen greeted each child with a smile and a hug. Lisa walked happily in the front door and immediately noticed the changes. The blackout curtains now had drawstrings and could be rolled up in the daytime – making it much more bright and cheerful. The windows were clean, the carpet was spotless, and Mrs Cohen's gramophone was now in the place of honour in the recess of the bay windows – the place where the piano had been and where it was no longer.

Lisa was stunned. Had the piano been damaged? Lisa saw Mrs Cohen glancing at her nervously.

Suddenly, a group of teenagers led by Johnny, Aaron and Günter jumped out from the hall and yelled, 'Surprise!'

Lisa was now totally confused. Before she could remind them that it wasn't her birthday, her friends circled around her, pushing her down the hall into the kitchen. The cellar door was standing open.

'Follow me, Maestro,' said Johnny. Lisa followed him down the stairs into the mouldy basement. The pickles and preserves had been moved – in their place was the sturdy old upright piano.

Mrs Cohen stepped carefully down two

stairs and peered into the room: 'It's not the Royal Albert Hall, but if you insist on playing through the bombings, at least you should play where it's safe.'

Lisa was speechless. When she recovered her manners she said, 'I don't know how to thank you.'

'You should thank them,' Mrs Cohen said, pointing to Johnny, Aaron, and Günter. 'They did all the work.' The boys took a bow. 'Now, be sure you practise! I would hate to think they brought such a heavy load down these stairs for nothing!'

Lisa kissed Johnny and Günter, then gave a romantic smooch to Aaron, and the room broke out in whistles. The younger boys poked their heads in from the kitchen door, adding, 'Play something, Lisa!'

Everyone crowded around the piano, pushing aside tins of peas and carrots and cleaning supplies to get a better look.

Lisa decided on something playful, an impromptu of Schubert. She hadn't played in a while, and she was nervous at first. She stretched her fingers, shaking them out above the keys, then launched into the piece.

One of the 11-year-olds blurted out:
'Go, Lisa!'

After the first few chords, Lisa called
out loudly up the stairs, 'Oh, Mrs Cohen! You
had the piano tuned! Thank you so much!' Mrs
Cohen beamed back; Lisa could only imagine how
complicated it must have been, with the rationing
and the lack of money and the million other repairs
that the matron was responsible for. She finished
the short Schubert piece with a flourish and
everyone clapped. Looking around at the familiar
faces, she realised how deeply she had missed her
Willesden Lane family.

'All right, no more time for fooling around,
everyone! I have posted the chore lists, so let's
get to work!' the matron said forcefully, and the
teenagers boisterously pushed each other up
the stairs.

Mrs Cohen came over to Lisa as she was
closing the piano. 'Miss Jura? Please come to my
room before dinner, I want to talk with you about
something.'

'Yes, ma'am,' Lisa said, worried as always
by the formal tone of the matron's voice. Had she

done anything wrong? Maybe she shouldn't have kissed Aaron in front of everyone.

Lisa prayed the meeting with Mrs Cohen would have something to do with her music and would not be any bad news about the many things she always worried about – her parents, Rosie and Sonia. She knocked on the door nervously.

'Come in, please,' the matron said.

The room had been rearranged since the bombing, and all the breakable clutter had been removed, making it as sparse as the Quaker house. Mrs Cohen was sitting on the bed; in front of her was an open copy of the *Evening Standard* newspaper.

'I've been saving this to show you,' Mrs Cohen said, pointing to a small announcement in the middle of the page.

It read: 'Auditions for scholarships and study at the Royal Academy of Music. Applications being accepted until 1 April. Open to all students with a proficiency in musical performance of the classical repertoire.'

The London Royal Academy? Lisa felt a

rush of emotion. This was where the great musicians studied; this was where Myra Hess herself had studied! Could she possibly qualify for such a school?

'Would you like to apply for an audition?' Mrs Cohen asked.

'Would they let a refugee girl go to the Royal Academy?' Lisa asked.

'Why shouldn't they? There's no shame in being a refugee, young lady,' Mrs Cohen scolded.

Lisa was overwhelmed, not just with the possibility of an audition, but with gratitude toward the matron. She could hardly believe that someone was actually looking out for her, helping her with decisions about her future. She was so used to having only herself to rely on since she'd said goodbye to her parents two years before.

'But I haven't studied in three years.'

'You've been practising, haven't you?'

'I haven't had a teacher, maybe it's all been wrong,' she said, suddenly feeling terribly insecure.

'Don't you trust your ability, dear?'

Lisa's eyes were shining, but she was tongue-tied.

'I take it you do. Are you interested?'

The phrase 'make something of yourself' was centre stage in her mind. She knew this would make her mother so proud. It would be the first thing she would tell her when she saw her. An audition at the Royal Academy!

'Yes, ma'am. I am,' she answered firmly.

'Good. Now, let's go to dinner.'

Mrs Glazer carried out the steaming platters of meat, and the crowded table clapped in appreciation. She paused before rushing back to the kitchen and said, 'It's so nice to have all of you back again. If truth be told, I missed your mess. It's been downright boring without you!' Everyone laughed.

Mrs Cohen held up a small pile of correspondence. 'Not many letters are getting through, I'm afraid, but I do have a few … Lewin, Kingman, Weisel, Jura, and Mueller.'

The letters were passed down the line to waiting hands, and Lisa took hers gingerly. The stamp had the words Republica de Mexico engraved on it, and she didn't recognise the name on the return address. She quickly stuffed it in her pocket.

'Aren't you going to read it?' Aaron asked.

146

'It's not polite, I'll wait until after dinner,' she bluffed. But the truth was that Lisa was always terrified when she received a letter. The news was never good and brought so many disappointments. She resolved to enjoy what was left of the Sabbath dinner before learning what worrying things awaited her.

After the children devoured dessert Aaron whispered, 'Get your coat, let's go next door.'

Lisa nodded and disappeared upstairs.

The convent door was open. Aaron had brought a blanket and a candle, and they made themselves comfortable in one of the rooms in the front of the building.

'Will you read it to me?' Lisa asked in a small voice, handing him the letter. She was grateful to be in his presence.

He opened the envelope with care; the blue airmail paper was covered with neat handwriting and dated 20 March 1941, only the week before.

'Dear Lisa, My name is Alex Bronson. I am your brother-in-law Leo's cousin. I am writing to you to see if you have any information regarding

Leo and Rosie, as we have lost contact with them since their escape to Paris.'

'Paris? They made it to Paris?' Lisa asked, relieved and worried at the same time.

Aaron continued reading: 'In case you haven't heard, Rosie and Leo pretended to be drunken Dutch tourists returning after a New Year's Eve in Vienna and successfully fooled the Nazi guards into letting them get on the train. They travelled to Antwerp, where my father helped smuggle them to France. We got a postcard a month later, saying that they'd got married, then our visas came through, and we left for Mexico. That was eight months ago and we have had no news of them since.'

Lisa let out a sob.

Aaron handed her his handkerchief.

'Go on.'

'We pray Leo and Rosie have been able to leave France because we are receiving news that Jews are no longer safe there; deportations have begun to camps in Poland. We are making inquiries to the Red Cross but have got nowhere. We are hoping that you may have received some word of them and could get in contact with us, since they do not have our address in Mexico.'

Lisa shivered as she thought about her beautiful sister and tried to conjure up an image of her and Leo safe somewhere. Were they hiding somewhere? Had they escaped?

Her head kept spinning.

Her thoughts were interrupted by the air raid siren sending out its shrill call. Aaron and Lisa waited in each other's arms until they saw the procession of lanterns and footsteps from next door, heading for the convent.

Maybe it was the comfort of the Willesden Lane reunion that buoyed Lisa's spirit, or the time spent in Aaron's arms. Whatever it was, Lisa was humming the Grieg Concerto to herself when the all-clear signal sounded a few hours later.

Chapter 17

At the factory, Lisa decided it was time to include
Mr Dimble and Mrs McRae in her 'other life', and
she asked if she could work a shorter shift (with a
cut in pay, of course) to allow extra time to
practise. She showed them the newspaper clipping
with its impressive 'Royal Academy' logo and told
them of her plans to apply for an audition.

'My, my, that's very posh,' Mr Dimble said,
somewhat sceptical.

'Have a heart, Raymond, you've let other
people have shorter shifts before, I've seen you!
Why not let her off to practise the piano?'
interjected Mrs McRae.

Mr Dimble shook his head as though it were
way beyond his understanding.

'Three o'clock it is, then, but no slacking off
before then, my girl!'

'Thank you so much,' Lisa called after him

as he headed down the line to intercept a cartload of fabric.

After work, Lisa went straight to the Royal Academy of Music, where a polite secretary reached behind her for a packet of papers, handing the mimeographed sheets to Lisa. 'The deadline for the application is next Friday. Please fill out your choice of repertoire and bring the completed form back to us.'

As she walked out, Lisa studied the young men and women who were rushing by her. She heard snatches of their conversations, which included words such as art and soul and beauty. It was all too wonderful.

Arriving home, Lisa ran to find Hans. 'I've got the application, come sit with me, so we can go over it.'

They got right to work, Hans sitting cross-legged on the sofa as she read: 'Applicants are advised to carefully select repertoire to display to best advantage the full range of their capabilities.'

'This is so fantastic!' he said, interrupting her, as excited as if it were his own audition.

'All repertoire must be performed by memory,' she continued. 'Well, of course!'

'That's obvious,' Hans echoed. 'Now … what are you going to play?'

Lisa continued reading: 'The applicant will be required to perform a work from each of the major stylistic periods in classical literature. First: Bach – choose a prelude or fugue from the *Well-Tempered Clavier*.'

Lisa thought for a second, then shouted: 'The D Minor!'

'Not a bad idea,' Hans agreed. 'All right, next.'

'A sonata by Beethoven,' she read. 'I could do the Thirty-two Variations!'

'It said a sonata,' Hans corrected her.

'Oh, I did the early A Major when I was in Vienna,' she offered, and hummed the opening phrase.

'Not strong enough. Don't forget the competition is going to be tough, you have to amaze them. What about the *Pathétique*?'

'I only just started it.'

'Then do you know the *Waldstein*?'

'Heavens no! I'd rather do the *Pathétique*!'

'The *Pathéthique* it is, then,' Hans said firmly.

Lisa kept reading: 'A major work by a romantic composer: Chopin, Schumann, Schubert, Brahms … That's simple, I'll do the Chopin Nocturne, the one that you like.'

'Not substantial enough.'

'But I'm really good at it!' Lisa said defiantly.

'Not possible.' Hans lost himself in thought for a moment. 'I know just the piece. It was written for you.' He got up, felt his way to the gramophone, and turned it on to warm up. He pointed to the stack of records.

'Find me the Rubinstein recording. I want you to hear Chopin's Ballade in G Minor.'

Obediently she found it and guided the needle into place. They lay back on the sofa and listened to the heartbreaking and passionate ballade.

'It's everything that you are, Lisa. You must play it,' Hans commanded.

They listened as Rubinstein furiously attacked the difficult and thunderous chords of the coda.

'Do you think I can do that?' Lisa's eyes were wide in amazement.

Hans looked momentarily worried. 'I forgot about the coda. Do you think it's too difficult?'

The very words 'too difficult' sparked Lisa's competitive spirit. Wasn't she Lisa Jura, the prodigy of Franzensbrückenstrasse, the one who had made all the neighbours proud? What would Mama say if she missed her chance because a piece was 'too difficult'? She listened to the roiling passion in Rubinstein's notes, nodded to herself, and said simply, 'Yes, this is the piece.'

Lisa went about learning the notes in a methodical way, and day by day she started getting the feel of the Chopin and Beethoven pieces into her hands.

Her favourite break from practising came after dinner, when she, Aaron, Günter and Hans got their turn at the record player. Mrs Cohen had imposed strict rationing of gramophone time after fights had broken out about the choice of music.

Johnny's favourite record was by Glenn Miller. After working his 24-hour shift at the fire station, he cherished his 24 hours off at the hostel, when he would wait for the trombone solo and lift his head for a few minutes from the papers in front of him. The rest of the time he scribbled endlessly in his notebooks. Occasionally he showed a poem to Lisa, who thought them deeply evocative.

The younger children loved to sit on Johnny's huge shoes and have him lift them up with his legs as he continued to write in his notebook all the while. Ever since Lisa had said how much she liked his poems, he had become more accepted by her friends. She encouraged him to share his work with the rest, but he resisted, saving his poetry for Lisa alone.

When it was time for Lisa's turn at the gramophone, she and Aaron listened for the millionth time to Arthur Rubinstein's recording of Chopin's ballade, as she laid her head against his shoulder. (Gramophone time was difficult for Günter, who had seen Gina only once since everyone else had moved back to Willesden Lane.) If they were lucky, there would be no air raid siren, and they could spend a magical thirty minutes floating in the beauty of music.

Lisa listened carefully, but listening to a recording wasn't the same as having a teacher. If only the professor could be here to help, she thought. Yet it wasn't really the professor she yearned for, it was her mother. Some nights she would put her head on the keyboard and cry, 'Mama, why can't you be here to help me?'

Chapter 18

Lisa's persistent practising was an inspiration for the others. In the autumn, Edith enrolled in a shorthand course, determined as well 'to make something of herself.' Günter begged his boss, Mr Steinberg, to make good on his statement that he was 'crucial to the war effort' and received a promotion to the accounting department. Hans enrolled in a course to become a physical therapist and brought home braille anatomy books to study. And Johnny wrote more and more poetry, declaring that Lisa's music had convinced him to become a writer after the war.

Only Aaron, it seemed to Lisa, didn't join in the 'hard work brigade.' He showed up late several times a week and had to throw pebbles at the third-floor window so Günter would come down and let him in.

Through it all was the constant threat of

the bombings. The headlines would scream: '1,000 dead in One Hellish Night!' Then the next day, the retaliation: 'RAF Flyboys Batter the Ruhr'. Back and forth the destruction went.

In the midst of the chaos, Lisa kept to her disciplined schedule, practising and practising. She dedicated the next two months to sight-reading and fundamentals. Every night, after a long day at the factory, Lisa would hurry through her afternoon practice and, after a quick dinner, go back to the basement for the dreaded hour of instruction.

Hans was in charge of sight-reading. Since he had memorised every note of his own sheet music, he would instruct Aaron to choose a piece that Lisa hadn't seen before but which he knew perfectly.

'All right, look at the key signature and think ahead one measure. Ready? Go!' Hans clapped his hands once and off she went.

'Pretty funny, huh? A blind guy teaching you sight-reading!' Hans yelled over the music.

Music theory was Aaron's talent. He finally admitted to Lisa that he had studied the violin in Mannheim and had learned the basics of dominants, subdominants, and chord inversions. Science came easily to him, and he patiently digested and explained the principles of harmony.

'I wish I had known that before,' she marvelled. They would lie together on the couch in the living room, Glenn Miller blaring from the radio, and she would guess her way through the chord changes as the swing music filled the air.

Solfeggio was a trial for everybody. Lisa's singing voice wasn't particularly inspiring, and 'Do, re, mi, fa, sol, la, ti, do' wasn't a very pleasing tune. On behalf of the entire hostel, Edith finally insisted that 'Do, re, mi' be a 'basement only' activity.

One day, unexpectedly, Gina arrived at the hostel. 'I'm back!' was all she said in explanation, and took off chatting as much as always. She had managed to get a job as a beautician and gave up her nanny job in Richmond to return to her friends at 243 Willesden Lane. They were all glad to see her, especially Günter, who walked around with a moony grin for days. Gina confided to Lisa that Günter's smile made combing strangers' hair worth the step down in status. In no time, the two girlfriends were back sharing late-night confidences about life and love. Most nights, Gina lay face up on the bed, smiling from ear to ear, while Lisa coiled on her side, lamenting Aaron's bad-tempered streak. His attitude problem had got worse.

One evening, the argument between Mrs Cohen and Aaron was particularly heated. Whether it was the new edict she had received from Bloomsbury about stricter rules for curfew or Aaron's insolent attitude, her patience had finally run out.

'If you come back after curfew, you're not to come back at all.'

'Fine, have it your way,' Aaron said, and went into the basement to let off steam. He tried to get Lisa's sympathy – to no avail.

'Mrs Cohen is right, you idiot! You've got to be more serious. You're always fooling around,' Lisa lectured.

'You're sounding awfully high and mighty!' Aaron said, and turned and walked out.

Lisa went back to practising but after a few minutes found herself filled with regret and ran upstairs to the living room to find Aaron and apologise.

He was nowhere to be found, so she returned to the basement and her Bach.

The next night, Lisa was devastated when Aaron still had not returned. Lisa lay on her bed, contrite and worried. 'It's all my fault,' she moaned.

Gina looked on. 'Don't worry, he used to do this lots of times before you came. He'll be back.'

But Aaron didn't come back the next night, or the night after. Lisa lay on her bed at the call for lights-out, her body racked by coughing.

'Maybe you should stop practising for a while, Lisa. It's too cold down there,' Gina suggested, concerned.

'It's just a cough, it will go away, don't worry.'

'If it doesn't go away soon, we won't get any sleep,' Gina said, only half joking.

On the third night, the telephone in the hallway rang, and the girls heard Mrs Cohen's footsteps on the stairs.

'Lisa?' the matron called. 'It's Aaron Lewin on the telephone.'

Lisa jumped up and ran downstairs, grabbing the receiver. 'Aaron, Aaron, are you all right?'

161

Gina crept down the stairs and listened to her friend as she clutched the telephone to her ear.

'What? For how long?' Lisa cried out, alarmed. 'Wait, wait, don't hang up! Aaron? Aaron?' she shouted. The receiver went dead in her hand.

'He only had a one-minute call,' she said in disbelief to the matron and Gina as they approached.

'What happened?' they asked in unison.

'Aaron's been arrested! And sent to the Isle of Man – as an alien!'

'Oh, my God, for how long?' Gina asked.

'I d-don't know,' Lisa stammered.

Mrs Cohen took the receiver and hung it back on the hook. 'It was bound to happen to him sooner or later. You have to admit he was asking for it.'

As tears sprang to Lisa's eyes, Mrs Cohen put her arm around the distraught teenager. 'It won't be forever. Now, go upstairs, dear, try to get some sleep.'

Lisa disentangled herself from Mrs Cohen's awkward embrace, ran up the staircase, and threw herself on the covers of her ice-cold bed. Her sobs turned into a fit of coughing.

Gina stood over her friend, worried. 'Why don't I see if Mrs Cohen could make you some hot water and lemon or something?'

'He doesn't deserve it! Why would he deserve it? She must hate him.'

'She didn't mean anything. Of course he doesn't deserve it.'

'It's all my fault!'

'Why is it your fault? Lots of the boys are getting picked up. Look at Paul!' Gina said with as much sympathy as she could muster at that time of night.

Lisa kept mumbling to herself, not listening. 'It's all my fault. If only I hadn't been so mean, he wouldn't have left.'

'It's not your fault, and, besides, Paul said it wasn't so bad in the camp, remember?' Gina added.

'What do you know about it?' Lisa exploded, jumping out of bed and slamming the door behind her.

How was she going to live without Aaron?

December was miserable for Lisa. She practised as hard as ever, but the relentless cold had no warm embrace at the end of the evening. Aaron sent several postcards, apologising for being so careless, but his brief words made her miss him even more.

Lisa's cough got worse; it was so bad that sometimes Mrs Cohen could hear it through the closed door of the cellar. One night, as Mrs Cohen stood at the top of the stairs and listened to the alarming sound, she got an idea. She went to the telephone and made a call.

The following evening, as Lisa was playing a lyrical passage from the *Pathétique*, she heard a knock at the door. It opened slightly and a familiar face poked through the opening.

'Lisa? May I come in?' said Mrs Canfield.

'Oh, hello!' Lisa said, surprised. 'Yes, please, come on down.'

Mrs Canfield stepped carefully down the steps, followed by Johnny, who was carrying a small, old-fashioned coal-burning stove. Lisa recognised it from her house on Riffel Road.

'I can't accept this,' Lisa protested.

'Nonsense,' said the Quaker lady. 'You'll

catch your death down here.'

'What will you use at home?'

'I have plenty of jumpers and coats. I don't need it.'

'I really appreciate it, but I just can't,' Lisa insisted. 'You can and you will,' Mrs Canfield said in an unyielding tone.

Lisa finally relented. 'Thank you,' she said gratefully. She hadn't wanted to admit how weak she had been feeling of late, and the warmth certainly would help.

Johnny lit the stove, and when he was sure it was functioning properly, stood up and handed her a folded sheet of paper. She opened it quickly, saw it was a poem, and smiled. 'Thank you, Johnny, I'll keep it on the piano to inspire me!'

'Be well, be warm!' Johnny called out on his way back up the stairs.

'Would thee mind if I stayed and listened?' Mrs Canfield asked.

'Oh, yes, please do,' Lisa replied.

Mrs Canfield pulled out the knitting bag she had brought, leaned back in her chair, and smiled.

'Lisa – what a comfort your beautiful

music is.'

An hour later, earlier than usual, the air raid siren went off. Usually the all-clear siren would sound several hours later, but this night was an exception. Hour after hour, the scream of the bombers came over them: no amount of pounding from the basement could chase the noise away. Lisa began to cough and couldn't stop, so she huddled by the stove under a blanket next to Mrs Canfield, who put her arm around her. Suddenly tired of being brave all the time, Lisa began to cry.

'What is wrong, my dear?' Mrs Canfield asked.

'Sometimes I miss my family so much that I feel I can't go on ... I can't go on without them. I don't even know why I should go on without them.'

Mrs Canfield hugged the trembling girl tight. 'It is not for thee to decide,' she said. 'Ultimately, God is in charge of our world. We have been placed here to do His will. I believe it is His will for thee to play your music. I hear a great truth in it.'

'My mother told me to always hold on to my music.'

'You must go forward with that in your heart, Lisa. Listen to your beloved mother.'

Finally, the all-clear blared, and Mrs Canfield looked at her watch. It was five in the morning. She helped Lisa up the stairs, and they walked out of the hostel into the bitter-cold dawn. Willesden Lane had been spared, but it seemed as though the rest of London was burning. Were the Nazis coming? Lisa wondered in a sudden delirium. She felt herself go limp.

The next thing she remembered was waking up in her bunk bed as Gina handed her a hot cup of chicken soup.

'You're awake! You're awake … oh, Lisa, we were so worried!' Gina cried, and ran out to spread the word.

Mrs Cohen arrived upstairs in an instant. 'You gave us quite a fright, dear,' she said with a slightly scolding tone. 'The doctor has confined you to bed rest for the next week; he says you have a bad bronchitis.'

'A what?' Lisa cried with alarm, not understanding the word.

'Bronchitis, a very bad cough. You're not to get up.'

'But I have to practise,' Lisa said.

'Not until you're better, that's an order.'

Gina was anxious to get her turn. She wanted to tell Lisa everything that was going on. 'You've been asleep for two whole days. You've missed everything!' she blurted out.

'Gina!' Mrs Cohen interrupted. 'Let Lisa rest, please.'

'No, Mrs Cohen, I want to know what's going on. Have the Nazis come?' she asked fearfully.

'The Nazis? No, silly! The Yanks are coming! You slept through the bombing of Pearl Harbor!'

'Pearl what?' Lisa asked, totally confused.

'The Americans have joined the war,' the matron explained. 'We'll tell you all about it later, dear.'

Suddenly, Gina hung her head and started to cry.

'What's wrong, please tell me!' Lisa asked.

'Hush, Gina, we must let Lisa rest,' said Mrs Cohen.

'It's Johnny,' Gina said, paying no attention to the matron.

'Johnny? What has happened?'

'Gina!' Mrs Cohen repeated sternly.

'Please tell me. Is he dead?' Lisa whispered.

'He's been badly hurt. A wall gave way in a building where he was helping to put out a fire. He is fighting bravely in the hospital and wants to be remembered to all of us, and to you especially, Lisa,' Mrs Cohen explained.

'He may lose his legs, though,' Gina added sadly.

Tears streamed from Lisa's eyes. 'Oh, no! Can I go and see him?' she asked.

'You are not to get out of bed,' the matron said firmly.

Lisa turned away from them to control her emotions. What a terrible thing this war is, she thought as she prayed for her friend.

Chapter 19

Two weeks of bed rest cured Lisa's fever, but her cough lingered. The audition date was fast approaching, so despite Mrs Cohen's reservations, she resumed a modified practice schedule.

The week before the audition, Lisa skipped her Monday-evening practice and went to see Johnny in the hospital. Johnny, pale and visibly thinner, had been confined to his bed and the head nurse told Lisa that her visit would have to be kept short.

He smiled when she approached, and she kissed him on the forehead.

'So are you ready?' he asked.

'For what?' she joked, as if she didn't know that everyone was counting down the hours to the audition.

'What will you play first?'

'The Chopin.'

'I have a request,' Johnny said gravely. 'When you play the Chopin, will you think of me?'

'Only if you give me another poem,' she teased.

Johnny put his head back slowly, closed his eyes, and began reciting softly:

'Tell me, what does God hear?

I have despaired of prayers with words

All of my prayers are your music.'

Lisa took his huge hands in her own. 'Of course I'll think of you, Johnny. I only wish I could play it for you right now.'

'You don't have to, all I have to do is close my eyes and I can hear it.'

Lisa kissed him gently and left.

With three days to go before the audition, Lisa was little good to Mrs McRae or Mr Dimble at the factory; she would fret about her playing and chatter nervously about her insecurities.

'I'll be up against students from the finest families in England,' she complained. 'And I don't even have a decent dress to wear.'

'That's a shame, isn't it,' Mrs McRae commented dryly.

Lisa realised with remorse how frivolous she must sound to this woman who had lost her husband in the war, and tried to get to work with no further complaints.

So it was with surprise that Lisa came to work the next morning and found a package, tied with recycled string, sitting on her chair.

'What's this?' she asked.

Several of the other ladies stood up and gathered around, saying nothing.

Mrs McRae looked up from her work with a mischievous grin, as if she didn't understand the question.

So Lisa picked it up and unwrapped it carefully. She pulled out a beautiful dark blue dress. 'Mrs McRae, you didn't …' Stunned, Lisa held up the elegant new dress and the ladies around her clapped.

'Very fancy, that is, Mrs McRae!' a co-worker said.

'Next thing you know, you'll be seamstress

to the queen!'

Mrs McRae smiled proudly. 'That'll impress 'em, I hope.'

'Oh, thank you! Thank you!' Lisa threw her arms around the woman.

The Saturday before the audition, Lisa was practising alone in the cellar when she heard a familiar whistling coming from the kitchen. It was the Grieg! She leapt up.

Could it be? Had Aaron miraculously come back to wish her luck? She ran to the top of the stairs only to find Günter! She tried to hide her disappointment as he laughed at her confusion and handed her a letter from Aaron.

She tore open the letter and raced quickly through his words. Aaron was uncharacteristically positive and convinced that he would be released soon.

He urged her on: 'Know that I love you and concentrate on the audition. I'll be thinking of you every moment.'

She reread the last line a second time, filled with joy, and then threw herself with added fervour back into the Beethoven.

On the day of her audition Lisa was surprised to see Günter waiting on the pavement.

'I'm going with you,' he said cheerfully. 'The hat factory has given me the day off.'

'Günter, you don't have to, I'll be fine.'

'Of course I do,' he said. 'I'm going to quiz you on the way.'

As they rode the train, Günter thumbed through the pages of the textbook, lobbing question after question.

Lisa hadn't really felt nervous until they arrived at the entrance to the Royal Academy of Music. She was once again overwhelmed by the grandeur of the building. She saw the large group of well-dressed English teenagers and their parents and felt the bottom drop out of her stomach. She could feel the atmosphere of intense competition enveloping the courtyard. She had known she would be up against a number of young and talented musicians, but she hadn't imagined how many.

The boys looked cool and confident. The

girls wore simple, elegant black dresses, and emitted a collective glow of beauty and confidence. But what made Lisa feel most apart from the others wasn't the fact that she had a blue dress and not a black one. It was that she was the only aspiring artist in line on this important day who wasn't accompanied by her parents.

Don't worry, Mama, she said silently. I know you're here.

Lisa and twenty other students were taken to a small classroom on the third floor, where she was handed a pencil and a test booklet and told she had one hour to complete the music theory portion of the exam. The pages were filled with endless questions. Nervous that she was spending too much time on each, she began to speed through them in a flurry. There were questions she couldn't answer, but then there were many she could, and she alternated between the feeling that she was doing brilliantly and the fear that she was failing miserably. She answered the questions so fast that she finished the exam early but felt too scared to go back and check things, afraid she would get confused.

'Pencils down,' the monitor said finally, then

Lisa was taken to a practice room with an upright piano, where she was tested on pitch and solfeggio by a serious young man. She sang the intervals as asked and did her best to name the notes as the man struck them on the keyboard.

'Thank you,' he said when it was over, not giving any hint of how she had done. 'Please wait in the hallway outside the auditorium on the first floor.'

A young woman with a clipboard came by and told Lisa that she would be sixth in line for the performance section of the audition. She was relieved to know the order. At least she wouldn't have her heart in her throat each time the auditorium doors swung open and a new student was called.

When the woman with the clipboard called out her name, Lisa stood up as proudly as she could, disguising the sudden pounding of her heart, and walked through the double doors.

Her knees were weak as she walked down the corridor of the cavernous auditorium toward the stage, where a beautiful Steinway grand piano stood waiting. In the tenth row of the otherwise empty hall, three judges sat with impassive expressions.

She climbed the stairs, walked over to the piano, and bowed to the judges. She had planned to begin with the Ballade, in order to dazzle them from the beginning, but with the pounding of her heart terrorising her so, she decided to switch to the Beethoven. Maybe the steady march of the opening chords would calm her down.

'What would you like to play first?' the male judge on the left called out.

'Beethoven's Piano Sonata in C Minor, Opus Thirteen, Number Eight,' Lisa replied.

'The *Pathétique*,' the other man said, jotting down a note in the book in front of him.

She adjusted her weight on the piano bench, tested the pedals quickly to judge their spring, took a deep breath, and began.

The opening notes of the sonata were solemn, the tempo measured and deliberate. For Lisa, it was as heartfelt as the lighting of the candles on her parents' mantelpiece. She saw the care in her mother's hands as she kindled the flame of Shabbat, and relived the warmth of the glowing dining room in the harmonies of the dramatic chords.

Her hands flew lightly into the trills and arpeggios, speeding up and down the keyboard. She imagined the energy was like the preparations for the Sabbath meal. She saw the playfulness of her sister Sonia scurrying in and out with the plates – how fast she went on her excited little legs as the high notes tinkled and twirled through the acoustical perfection of the hall.

In the majestic simplicity of the notes, Lisa's hands searched for just the right touch to convey the poignant melancholy that lay within her.

'Thank you,' she heard between the notes near the end of the first movement. She suddenly realised that the judges had let her go on for ten whole minutes.

'Perhaps you could play your prelude and fugue next.'

She wanted to say, 'No, no, you must hear the Chopin!' But she bowed graciously and began Bach's Fugue in D Minor. She thought she was doing pretty well when the woman's thin voice pierced her concentration.

'Thank you,' said the small lady in the dark suit. 'And what have you prepared from the

Romantic period?'

'I will play Chopin's Ballade in G Minor, Opus Twenty-three, Number One.'

As with the Beethoven, the Chopin opened slowly and majestically. But then Chopin opened Lisa's heart with his romantic, interlaced melodies. Here was a composer who reached into the furthest recesses of Lisa's soul and stirred her deepest yearnings.

Lisa's mother had told her that in this ballade, Chopin was crying for the loss of his native Poland – at having to flee war and destruction, never to return. It was a tribute to his lost homeland. Lisa's fingers sang her own nostalgic tribute – to Vienna, now lost to her, and to her parents and Rosie, and even Sonia, so far from her.

She laid her heart bare as her fingers moved almost with no conscious effort. Lisa's strong but delicate fingers raced up and down the keyboard as she expressed the passionate yearnings for her future life – her growing feelings for Aaron, her prayer for Johnny's recovery, and her belief in the beauty of a world someday without war.

Another 'Thank you' broke into her

reverie, and she realised with alarm that she had played the entire piece without being interrupted. Maybe they had tried to stop her and she hadn't heard them.

She raised her head and looked out. The male judges were writing in their books, and the tiny woman nodded her head politely.

She scoured their faces for a reaction but found none.

'That is all, you may go,' was all she got by way of response, so she bowed politely and walked off the stage.

Günter was waiting in the hallway. 'How was it? How did you do?' he asked, anxious for the news.

'I did everything I could. I gave it my all. We all did, Günter!'

Chapter 20

February became March, but the weather in the spring of 1942 remained bitterly cold. Lisa started working overtime at the factory – as much to do her patriotic duty as to distract herself from the agony of waiting for the results of the audition.

She trudged down the block every morning, passing the same newsboy, and read the daily ration of gloomy news. It was true the Americans had given everyone a huge boost in morale, but the news from Europe continued to be grim – frightening rumours were circulating at the synagogue about the massive deportations of all Jews from Europe.

Delivery of the post at dinner was a sad time, since most of the children had stopped receiving letters from their parents in Europe. They had now transferred their expectations to waiting for Lisa's answer from the Royal Academy of Music.

'Lisa Jura?' Mrs Cohen said one Friday night at the Shabbat meal, holding up a letter. 'It's from the London Royal Academy of Music.'

Lisa stared at it, paralysed.

'Would you like me to open it?' said Mrs Cohen.

Lisa nodded. She had wanted to wait, to be alone, but she knew instinctively that she must share the news, good or bad, with everyone.

Mrs Cohen opened the letter, unfolded the thick, elegant stationery and read: 'The Associated Board of the London Royal Academy of Music is' – here Mrs Cohen paused to take a breath – 'pleased to inform Miss Lisa Jura that ...'

There was a scream at the end of the table from a young boy, who had a hand slapped over his mouth quickly.

'... she has been accepted into the scholarship programme for the study of the pianoforte. Please report ...'

Lisa was swarmed and enveloped by kisses, hugs, and thumbs-up signs, and those who couldn't get close enough to give one started to clap. She was a hero, and the children of Willesden Lane

182

desperately needed a victory.

She walked up to Mrs Cohen and put her arms around the matron. 'I never would have even known about the audition if it weren't for you. How can I ever thank you?'

'You have thanked me. You've brought honour to this house,' Mrs Cohen replied. 'We all need to dream, and tonight, everyone is living their dream through you.'

To add to Lisa's euphoria, Aaron was released the following week from detention camp. He showed up at 243 Willesden to help celebrate Lisa's triumph.

'Where are you taking me?' Lisa demanded in a friendly tone.

'We're going to celebrate, and that's all I'm saying,' was his answer.

Lisa ran upstairs, putting on her new pleated skirt and a chic blue blouse, topped by a stylish felt hat, and met him in the foyer. He whistled his approval, and off they went.

They jumped on a double-decker bus and were having so much fun, they almost missed their stop – the Parliament building, or what was left of it after the bombing.

'What are we doing here?' Lisa asked, somewhat disappointed.

'Just wait, you'll see.'

'This better be good!' she teased.

Finally an old gentleman arrived and waved. 'Hello, Mr Lewin!' he said, shaking Aaron's hand. 'Let's go!' The man unlocked a door and led them to some narrow stairs.

'Come on, hurry up!' Aaron said, and they followed the man up and up the stairs.

'Are we there yet?'

'Keep climbing! You'll just have to trust me,' Aaron said.

When they reached the top, Lisa saw it – a giant clock with its inner workings and huge bells.

'It's Big Ben!' Aaron exclaimed.

'I can't believe it!' Lisa cried delightedly.

They were high above London, and the city stretched out below them, the House of Commons, the great dome of St. Paul's, and the crowded, winding streets. The Thames flowed peacefully and disappeared into the distance. Lisa slipped her hand into Aaron's, but instead of taking it, he wrapped his arms around her, enveloping her in a kiss.

Then they stood, speechless, staring at the great panorama before them. The war, the bombs, and the destruction seemed to disappear, too.

At that moment, Lisa dared to have hope. Hope that the war could be won, hope that she'd see her family again, and hope that if she studied hard enough, she could become what she had always dreamed – a concert pianist.

As she stared at the thousands of buildings and homes laid out before her, she imagined she was staring at a thousand faces – the faces in a concert hall, the faces in the daydream she used to have on the tram in Vienna. She imagined the elegantly dressed audience waiting for her to begin. She could hear the hush and feel the anticipation as she sat in front of the nine-foot grand piano.

She saw Aaron was also dreaming of faraway things. But he wasn't staring at the horizon, he was looking down at a group of British soldiers gathered beneath Big Ben's tower.

Chapter 21

The reappearance of the crocuses in the spring of 1943 meant that another year had passed, but Lisa was so absorbed in her new studies that she hardly had time to read the corner chalkboard, which was plastered with encouraging headlines like: 'Allies Enter Naples and Kiev Liberated!'

The Royal Academy of Music had proved as exciting as she had hoped and as demanding as she had anticipated. In the autumn of 1942, her first year, she had been assigned a 'master teacher' and was surprised when she opened the door to the studio to find that it was the same small lady who had been on the jury at the audition. Her name was Mabel Floyd, a teacher with a very distinguished reputation.

That first year brought many other changes in Lisa's life. After a long struggle, Johnny had died, leaving a hole in the heart of the hostel. His internal injuries were more severe than any of them had known. She missed him terribly.

To add to her loneliness, Aaron enlisted in the Auxiliary Military Pioneer Corps as a paratrooper. After seeing the look in his eyes as he watched the soldiers from the tower of Big Ben, Lisa knew his announcement should come as no surprise.

On the night before he was to ship out, he came to the hostel, and Mrs Cohen kindly lent them her room for a few private hours to say goodbye.

When the evening was over, Lisa was crying so hard that she couldn't leave Mrs Cohen's room for the final glimpse of Aaron going out the door.

At first she wrote to him every day, then every week, but then she grew so busy that she wrote just once a fortnight. Aaron had done the same, as he was swept up in the life of the hardships of the parachute division. In the beginning his letters were detailed and enthusiastic, but after his first combat experience, they became more guarded; Lisa tried to read between the lines. What was it like? What had he seen? She didn't want to imagine.

The summer of 1943 brought the glorious news that the Bateses finally agreed that it was safe enough to allow Sonia to come and visit with her older sister in London.

When Lisa met Sonia at the train, she was surprised to see that Sonia was still thin and small for her 16 years.

'Are you getting enough to eat out in the country?' she asked.

'It's not like Mama's cooking, but don't worry, I'm trying to eat as much as I can.'

Lisa took Sonia to all of her favourite spots in her new city: at Buckingham Palace they strained for a glimpse of the princesses. When they walked past Big Ben, Lisa confided that she had been kissed on top of the bell tower.

At night, Sonia cried out for their mother in her sleep, and asked in the morning when Lisa thought they would see their parents and Rosie again.

'I don't know,' Lisa began, but seeing Sonia's mournful expression, she added, 'I'm sure it will be soon.'

Despite the rough moments, it was a

wonderful visit, and both sisters were distraught on Sunday afternoon when it was time to part once again. They vowed to keep writing often, especially if either heard any news of the family.

Just a few weeks after Sonia's visit, Lisa got a short letter from Leo's cousin in Mexico. Letters from Austria had stopped completely. Lisa ripped open this letter and scanned it quickly for news:

'Still haven't heard from Leo or Rosie, but we did get news that most Jews from Vienna have now been deported to detention camps in Poland. We have tried desperately to get word about our aunts and uncles there, but there are few ways to communicate from here in Mexico. Please write to us if you hear anything at all.'

In panic, Lisa brought this letter to Bloomsbury House, but neither they nor the Jewish Refugee Agency nor anyone else could answer their frantic appeals. All letters came back stamped 'Undeliverable,' and every attempt Lisa and the others at the hostel made to contact their parents was unsuccessful.

By 1943, Platz & Sons was making military

accessories – duffel bags, backpacks, mudguards, camouflage, all sewn from heavy green canvas. The work was harder than before, and Lisa's tired fingers began to feel the strain from the difficult, repetitive work.

The centrepiece of her week was her lesson with Mabel Floyd. After faithfully practising all that she had been assigned, she would appear enthusiastically at the master teacher's studio at 3.30pm on Thursdays.

'No, no, no,' Mrs Floyd interrupted Lisa after just a few beats. 'A trill is something light! Think of fairy dust, the tinkling of little bells. This sounds like a parade of army boots.'

Lisa rubbed the painful muscles of her right forearm and began again. The same results.

'Is there something else you need to tell me, dear?' The discerning teacher noticed the worry in her pupil's eyes.

Lisa had been reluctant to talk about her factory job with Mrs Floyd, but finally she described her arduous work. The teacher knew she was a refugee but hadn't known the details about the rigours of the assembly line.

'My, my, we'll have to do something about that,' was her brisk response. 'Go home and get some rest. I'll see you next week. There will be no assignment.'

At the end of the next lesson Mrs Floyd handed Lisa a handwritten letter. 'Take this to the Howard Hotel, the address is inside. They are looking for a pianist to entertain the soldiers. I believe the pay is reasonable and the work will be much more suitable.'

Lisa drew in her breath – a little gasp of delight. 'Oh, thank you! Thank you, Mrs Floyd.'

She floated several inches off the pavement all the way to the Howard Hotel, where she presented the letter to the manager, was shown the piano in the lounge, and was told she could begin the following week.

The next day at the factory was difficult; Lisa dreaded goodbyes.

Mr Dimble said, 'We're sorry to lose you, but good luck in show business.'

Lisa laughed and thanked him with a kiss on

the cheek that made the poor man blush.

The farewell to Mrs McRae was the hardest. 'I'll be reading the newspapers, searching for your name, Lisa. I'll be reading the arts section! Won't that set them a-titterin'.'

They hugged, and with no further ceremony Lisa left the life of the factory behind.

Chapter 22

The Howard Hotel was a bustling nightspot in the West End of London, with a large restaurant, a small ballroom with swing dances on Saturday nights, and 'entertainment in the lounge' the other six nights a week. Lisa posed for a photograph that was placed on an easel in the foyer: 'In the Oak Room, Lisa Jura, at the Piano'.

The first night, she chose the liveliest of Chopin's mazurkas and several of Mendelssohn's songs without words. She learned fast to avoid Bach and Beethoven. The crowd was appreciative, and so was the manager when he saw the patrons moving from the restaurant to the lounge.

'Play *Peg o' My Heart!*' someone yelled. 'No, play *I'll Be Seeing You!*'

Lisa smiled and tried to be charming, but she realised immediately that she had better find some new music. The next day, revelling in the wonder of having a free morning, she shopped near Tottenham Court Road for the favourite tunes of the day.

Her training in sight-reading really paid off, and soon the entire room was singing along with Lisa's spirited versions of the wartime hit parade. She played *We'll Meet Again* and *I'm Going to Get Lit Up* (*When the Lights Go Up in London*) and *When They Sound the Last 'All Clear'*.

Sometimes, when she saw a soldier in an RAF uniform, she would think of Aaron, although more with nostalgia than with the sting of longing she had first felt at their parting. But her worry about him intensified after the hostel received a telegram from the War Department advising them that Paul Goldschmidt had died. The telegram was addressed to Mrs Cohen, whose name had been filled in under 'Mother.' Mrs Cohen passed the telegram around the quiet dinner table, and saddened fingers touched the words 'valiantly gave his life in service …'

Mrs Glazer led the recitation of the prayer for the dead: 'May God remember the soul of Paul Goldschmidt who has gone to his eternal home …'

Paul's death was a blow to Lisa, not only because she missed his sunny smile but because it brought home the reality of the danger Aaron faced. The next day, she went to a small storefront shop that she often passed in Cavendish Square, where she had seen the sign: 'Star Sound Studios – send greetings to your loved ones far away!'

Even though the man was impressed by Lisa's rendition of Liszt's romantic *Liebestraüme*, adjusting the dials of the machine that cut the grooves into the 78rpm gramophone record, he still charged the full two pounds for the service. She left him the address of the paratroops division headquarters and inscribed the gold-and-white centre: 'Dear Aaron, with all my love, Lisa.'

One night, Lisa glanced out at the faces of the soldiers in the room and did a double take. For there was Aaron, completely unexpected, but, judging from the quickening of her pulse, more welcome than she had realised. She immediately stopped the piece she was playing, jumped up, threw her arms around him, and gave him a kiss.

'Sit right there! I'll join you at the break!'

When her work was done, she hurried to his table, where he sat alone in front of several emptied glasses.

'How about this place? Pretty fancy, don't you think?' she said.

'You played even more beautifully than your recording.'

'Oh, you got it!' Lisa cried out happily. 'Yes, thank you.'

'So, tell me everything!' she begged.

'You first.'

Lisa chattered about the hostel and the Howard Hotel, but the more she went on, the more she realised she was looking at a changed Aaron. He seemed so remote. 'Come on! Let's go for a walk,' she said, grabbing his hand.

They walked slowly up the dark and deserted avenues, heading for Hyde Park. The gates to the park were locked. Anti-aircraft guns stood as silent sentries behind the iron fence.

'Tell me about it, Aaron, what is it like?' Lisa asked gently, putting her arm on his shoulder.

In a monotone, he spoke about his regiment

196

and his training. He had joined a parachute company and had trained in a secret location. When he described the sensations of jumping out of a plane, he became briefly animated, like the Aaron she remembered. Then he fell silent again.

Lisa took his hand but didn't feel any warmth from it; his coldness frightened her. The closer she clung to him, the more distant she felt.

She wondered many things that she was afraid to ask. Were all soldiers like this? Was this what war did? Did it ruin everything? Where was the charming boy who had whistled the Grieg in her ear?

'What was it like when you landed somewhere?' she asked.

'You don't want to know,' he answered.

'Were you scared?'

'Of course, what do you think?'

'I don't know. That's why I'm asking. I want you to talk to me,' she begged.

Aaron stayed stubbornly silent, and finally Lisa stopped asking questions. After a while, he stopped abruptly, cocking his head toward the sky.

'What is it?' Lisa asked, alarmed.

'Shh,' he answered, standing perfectly still. Suddenly, before she could hear the sound that Aaron heard, the night was broken with the wail of air raid sirens.

'It's a V-2, hurry!' He took her hand and they ran together toward the underground station at Marble Arch. A wave of people rushed frantically from their blacked-out apartments and on to the pavements, carrying books, blankets, and hastily grabbed snacks. Aaron and Lisa ran after them, joining the hurried stream of Londoners running down the stairs into the safety of the tubes.

Down and down they went; Lisa stopped counting how many flights, grateful to be so deeply hidden from the approach of the German buzz bombs. When they arrived at the lowest floor, the cold-tiled platforms were already covered by rows of sleeping bodies; these were the early birds, who had taken to spending every night in the tubes, not waiting for the sirens.

People were everywhere – on the escalators, on the stairs, draped over benches and chairs. The more organised families had brought cots and blankets; the others lay huddled next to strangers for warmth. Lisa's mouth dropped at the sight of all the people; she had heard about these places, but had never been caught out at night in an air raid before.

With sleepy eyes, the tightly packed masses readjusted themselves to make room for the latecomers. Aaron found a wall to lean against, and the family next to them moved over a few inches with a nod of respect to his uniform. He took off his jacket and spread it underneath Lisa to shield her from the cold.

They were too far underground to hear the whine of the bombers, but every few minutes the ceiling gave off a layer of dirt and dust, shaken loose by the explosions above.

Aaron leaned his head against the dirty cement wall and stared at the sooty Londoners around him. 'People are a sorry lot, aren't they? We're nothing but cannon fodder.' His voice drifted off again into silence.

Lisa leaned her head on his shoulder and stared at the sleeping children next to them. An angelic two-year-old slept next to her leg, and as he tossed and turned, he yanked his blanket off, exposing his little pink legs. She pulled it back over him and realised as she did that tears were streaming from her eyes. She closed them and buried her face deeply into Aaron's shoulder.

The all-clear siren sounded several hours later and they dusted themselves off, making their way toward Willesden Lane. Overcome with exhaustion, Aaron and Lisa stood silently for a long moment in front of the hostel, watching the first light of dawn glowing in the eastern sky.

When they kissed goodbye, Lisa held him tightly, transported for a moment to the feelings she had the night when he first kissed her outside Mrs Canfield's house. The tighter she clung, the more she felt confused. Were these feelings merely the ghosts of her feelings from the past, or did she truly still care for him?

When she finally let go, Aaron smiled mysteriously and picked up his satchel.

'I'll write to you when I arrive,' he said, and walked slowly down the road.

She watched until he turned the corner and was sure she heard him whistling the first few bars of the Grieg.

'Lisa! Thank God!' Gina shouted when she saw Lisa tiptoe into the bedroom a few minutes later. 'We were worried sick! Where were you?'

'I was caught in an air raid,' Lisa answered, in no mood to share confidences. 'I had to spend the night in the underground.'

'We were really worried, they said a rocket fell near the hotel.'

Lisa said nothing as she put on her warm flannel nightgown and climbed into bed.

'Can I tell you something?' Gina asked, her voice filled with excitement.

Lisa waited silently, still lost in her upsetting thoughts.

'Günter and I are engaged. Look!' Gina exclaimed, holding out her left hand. There was a simple gold ring on her finger. 'This is just temporary,' she said, 'until he can afford the real one. He promised someday he'll buy me a diamond. You have to promise you'll play at our wedding! Promise?'

'Of course,' Lisa answered, smiling, disguising her sadness.

'Oh, thank you, thank you! I can't begin to

tell you how excited I am,' Gina went on, detailing the plans from beginning to end.

Lisa listened but her mind kept wandering to Aaron, trying to picture the images of happier times. Maybe when the war is over, he will change back into the Aaron I love, she told herself.

The next day, she felt grateful to escape her dark thoughts and return to her work entertaining the cheerful, raucous soldiers at the Howard Hotel.

Chapter 23

By 1944, the war was finally going their way. The Allies were heading for Rome and Russia had liberated Odessa. London was now crawling with soldiers – they were on the streets, in the theatres, and packed in at the Howard Hotel.

Tonight, Lisa was looking her best and decided to use the opportunity of such a large crowd to try out the Rachmaninoff prelude she had learned in preparation for her year-end recital.

The mysterious aura of the Rachmaninoff matched the mood of expectation. Soldiers' leaves had been cancelled abruptly; most of them knew they would be back on ships and planes the next day. The hush in the lounge was deeper than usual. After Lisa played the powerful ending, three soldiers approached, led by a lieutenant, carrying a carnation. He stepped forward and said:

'*Mademoiselle!* There is a gentleman who

wants to meet you.' The soldier had such a strong French accent and such charming determination that Lisa didn't feel the least bit like saying no. Besides, it was time for her break.

She followed them back to a table, where a tall man, with compelling dark brown eyes and a wonderfully direct expression stood up immediately. He held out his hand and she took it, assuming he wanted to shake, but he raised it to his lips gracefully and kissed it instead.

'C'était magnifique! Que vous êtes magnifique!'

'I'm sorry, I don't speak French,' Lisa said.

'Rachmaninoff!' he said, cupping both hands over his heart.

'Ah, so you know!' She beamed at him.

Then it was his turn to throw his hands in the air.

'You don't speak any English?' Lisa asked.

'His English is terrible,' said his friend, speaking for him. 'He's in the Resistance, fighting for the Free French. He's our captain.'

The captain then said something in a deep voice to his lieutenant, who turned to Lisa and translated.

'He says to tell you that you are the most beautiful woman he has ever seen.'

Intrigued by the aura of strength about the French captain, Lisa found herself believing it, just a little.

The captain pulled out his calling card and handed it to Lisa, looking in her eyes and saying a few words in French.

The lieutenant translated: 'He says you must promise to invite him if ever you give a concert. He says, no matter where he is, he will come.'

The next night, there was an unusual emptiness at the Howard Hotel. On her way back home, Lisa looked up at the sky and saw wave after wave of transport planes flying overhead. The Allied invasion of Europe had begun.

Lisa had been working toward the final, end-of-term recital that students gave in late June to the faculty and students of the Royal Academy of Music.

She arrived at her lesson with Mrs Floyd and played through the pieces in a run-through for the upcoming event. Mrs Floyd clapped appreciatively at the end, and Lisa took out her pencil and prepared to mark the music as usual with the new round of critiques. To her surprise, the teacher asked her to put her pencil away.

'Lisa, I don't have any notes today. It is time to trust yourself; you are ready to soar!'

After so many lessons where she had heard her playing dissected and analysed, this was wonderful news. Lisa would go to this recital and finally play 'what was in her heart.'

'One more thing,' Mrs Floyd said with a twinkle in her eye. 'It's time to think about your debut.'

Lisa was so stunned, she said nothing.

'Usually, a student's family helps toward the expenses of a debut, but because of your circumstances, the faculty has recommended that the Academy help in the arrangements.'

Lisa remained speechless.

'That is, if you would like a debut,' Mrs Floyd said, teasing.

Lisa leapt from her seat, crying, 'Of course I would!' and wrapped her arms around her instructor in an exuberant, spontaneous hug. 'I don't know how to thank you,' Lisa said, genuinely honoured.

'Oh, and one more thing. For the location of your debut … we are thinking of Wigmore Hall.'

Wigmore Hall! It was incredible. The moment she had dreamed about all her life was finally within her grasp.

Chapter 24

The June recital had gone off without a hitch, and Lisa settled into a summer and autumn of choosing and preparing a new repertoire for her debut. The Howard Hotel remained a popular nightspot, and now Günter took to joining Gina for a weekly Friday-night visit.

As winter came, the battles in Europe raged even more intensely, and it was decided to wait a season to rent Wigmore Hall for the debut. Rationing was severe and people's minds were on war, not music. January saw the Allies battling through a frozen Europe, taking back city after city from the Third Reich. Russia marched through Poland, and the United States and Great Britain obliterated Dresden in a firestorm.

When she heard there was a battle raging for Vienna, Lisa went to the synagogue and said a special prayer. Would her city disappear as

Dresden had?

Through the avalanche of news, the children of Willesden Lane waited. Waited for letters, waited for word. Straining for news from the deportation camps, where they knew their parents were waiting to be liberated.

Lisa tried mightily to centre herself in the music and her practice, and Mrs Floyd helped her perfect the repertoire for her debut.

In the middle of a passage, the door to the studio flew open and two excited girls poked in their heads.

'Hurry up! Haven't you heard?'

When Lisa lifted her hands from the keys they could hear the faraway bells – the pealing of Big Ben! Then the sounds gathered momentum – and were joined by the bells of the churches all throughout London.

Lisa ran to the window; people were running and shouting and jumping in the air. Union Jacks sprouted from every window, and horns were honking wildly.

Lisa had never seen Mrs Floyd move so fast, but there she was, leading a group of excited students down the spiral staircase and into the streets, where they joined the growing crowd. They boarded a packed trolley, which weaved through a sea of revellers wearing paper hats and waving noisemakers, headed for Buckingham Palace. When the trolley could no longer move, they got out and were pushed the remaining blocks to the Mall, where Churchill himself was addressing the throng.

Lisa was awestruck. She had heard his broadcasts, seen him on the newsreels and in the newspapers – but here he was in person, the man whose words had given strength to everyone during the dark years.

'God bless you all. This is your victory!' he roared into the microphone. 'There we stood alone, did anyone want to give in?' the prime minister thundered, his words echoing across the vast expanse.

'No!' The crowd shouted again.

'Were we downhearted?'

'No!'

'In all our long history we have never seen a greater day than this,' he said, waving his famous hat.

Then, when it seemed the crowd could not get any more excited, the king and queen and the princesses appeared on the balcony, waving as the crowds cheered.

The war in Europe was over! Hitler was dead! The Allies had taken Berlin! The horror was over – at least for the millions and millions of British who had fought so proudly and suffered so much.

Staring at the joy on people's faces, Lisa was suddenly overcome with a shiver of isolation and sadness. When would the war be over for her? Or for her friends at the hostel?

From the swirl of the crowd, Mrs Floyd and the other students reappeared and invited Lisa to join them for a victory dinner.

'Oh, thank you so much,' Lisa answered. 'But I think maybe I should celebrate with the others at home,' she said, suddenly not feeling at all in a celebratory mood.

'Are you sure?' her teacher yelled above the noisy crowd.

Lisa nodded her head and waved goodbye as two of the students grabbed Mrs Floyd by the hand, pushing the elegant English lady into a conga line that danced away from her. Lisa headed away from the raucous festivities.

At first, there were just rumours. Unsubstantiated rumours, impossible rumours, which spread like wildfire through the already broken hearts of the Jewish community. Place names like Treblinka, Bergen-Belsen, Nordhausen, Auschwitz and Theresienstadt were whispered from ear to ear.

Talk of mass graves, piles of bodies, unspeakable acts. Photos leaked out, of hollow-eyed people staring from behind barbed-wire fences, their bony bodies hardly able to stand.

Lisa couldn't read most of the articles about it in the newspaper. She couldn't bear to hear it when she was told. She had known the terror of the Nazis, seen Kristallnacht, but never could she have imagined what had transpired, unreported, behind Nazi lines.

The Red Cross, the Jewish Refugee Agency, and the U.S. Army began to post lists of concentration camp survivors as they were liberated, moved, and organised in camps for displaced persons.

Lisa flocked with the other desperate refugees to the agencies posting the lists. The pages were chaotic and disorganised, taped to walls in crowded hallways, put up as soon as beleaguered workers could type them, to help the frantic search of the heartbroken relatives.

She went every day to see if new lists had been compiled, going over and over the old ones with care. Seeing that there were no Juras on the list, Lisa looked for Leo's name. There were dozens of Schwartzes, but no Leos and no Rosies.

One day Günter found his mother's name on the list from a displaced persons camp near Theresienstadt. He spent the day writing hurried telegrams to make contact. When he returned to the hostel, he was so sensitive to the others' pain that he told only Gina about his news, feeling it was selfish to talk openly of his good fortune. But Mrs Cohen heard and spread the word, feeling it important that what little joy there was should be shared.

During those first months of searching, Lisa would often lie on her bed and stare at her parents' pictures and try hard to remember their faces. Sometimes, but only in a dream, she thought she could catch a glimpse of her mother's expression on Kristallnacht, when she had wiped the blood from her father's face. And she could sometimes see the smile her mother gave her when they would play together at the piano after her lesson with the professor.

'*Yisgadal v'yiskadash*' – 'May the great name of God be exalted'. Nightly, the prayers at the synagogues chanted the names of the departed.

One weekend afternoon, a familiar figure walked through the front door of the hostel. It was Aaron Lewin, carrying his Royal Air Force satchel and wearing the insignia of lieutenant.

Mrs Cohen was the first to recognise him. 'Aaron! How wonderful to see you. Come in, come in!'

'Is Lisa here?' he asked, direct as always.

'Yes, she's upstairs, please go on up.'

'Aaron!' Lisa yelled, leaping off the bed. 'It's so good to see you!' And it was good to see him again; he looked so mature, so sophisticated. She gave him a brief hug, but the feeling between them was distant – she had got no letters from him for many months.

'I was worried about you! Are you all right?'

'Never better,' he answered, but his expression said the opposite. 'This place looks like it needs some attention,' he continued, glancing at the cracked glass of the window. 'Maybe I should grab the toolbox.'

Lisa smiled and led him to the kitchen to find the matron. She knew that Aaron needed time to get his bearings.

They spent the day together. Lisa watched as Aaron tackled the mechanical things that badly needed fixing.

After lunch, Lisa felt it was time to broach the difficult question she had been waiting all morning to ask. 'Have you heard anything about your family, about your mother?'

'My mother is dead. So are my brothers,' he

answered, not adding any details.

'How?'

'I don't know. How would we ever know?'

'Then how are you sure they're dead?'

'We have to just assume it, don't we?' he said flatly, trying to shield himself from the pain of his words.

'How can you just assume it?' she said, starting to get upset.

'Lisa, you must be realistic. I think it's time you faced it. What are the chances any of them survived?'

'Am I supposed to give up hope? Is that what you're saying?' Lisa asked, trying to sound defiant. But her words came out halfhearted. Could it be possible that she would never see her parents or Rosie again?

As the long summer afternoon was ending, Aaron asked Lisa to come with him into the back garden. They walked to the hedge that separated the hostel from the convent next door. Lisa's heart was still heavy from the terrible realisations that were beginning to wash over her.

Aaron had his back to her as he said, 'I'll be

leaving for New York. I've managed a visa
for America.'

'Oh,' she said, with an involuntary gasp.

Still facing away from her, he continued:
'Will you come with me?'

Lisa was silent. Her world was fragmenting
around her; she was facing the loss of everyone she
held dear. Could she bear to lose Aaron even if she
knew her feelings had changed? She didn't know if
she had the strength to say no.

When Aaron turned around, he saw her
deep in troubled thought and knew her answer.

A week later, Aaron came to the hostel
before his final departure, bringing sweets and
cakes. He was trying to be positive and forward
looking, fighting, as they all were, for a reason to go
on. He had found his in the journey to America.

Lisa's reason? She didn't know. She could
only stand sadly on the steps of the hostel, next to
Günter and Gina, and wave goodbye.

Chapter 25

Gina and Günter made a handsome bride and groom. Their big day had finally arrived, and they celebrated at Willesden Lane.

Lisa had put on her brightest face for the happy occasion, a feat made easier because finally, her sister Sonia had been allowed to move to London. She had moved into the hostel the week before. The war was over, and the city was safe. Sonia was delighted to be near her older sister.

When the vows were over, Günter kissed his bride and stepped on the champagne glass to cries of '*Mazeltov!*' Then the assembly of well-wishers clapped and the music began.

Although still in no mood to play, Lisa had agreed, out of a sense of duty, to perform the first movement of the Grieg Piano Concerto. As the notes of the first few bars floated into the warm outdoor air, Lisa couldn't help but think of Aaron.

He had sent a congratulatory telegram. Although her feelings for him were no longer romantic, Lisa missed his presence terribly.

When she was finished, Günter gave a toast to 'all those missing today,' making special mention of Paul and 'Johnny King Kong'.

'May we remember the beauty of their gentle spirits and keep their memory in our hearts for the rest of our lives.'

Feeling the pall that had been cast by Günter's words, and not wanting the wedding day to turn sombre, Mrs Glazer hurried to bring out the cake. After the couple did a ceremonial cutting of the first piece, Günter announced formally what they had all assumed: that he and Gina would be heading for New York as soon as his mother joined them. Lisa hugged her friends warmly, and was gripped by the sadness of another goodbye.

Children were arriving at the hostel from the displaced persons camps of Europe, where they had been brought from the hell of Bergen-Belsen, Auschwitz and Dachau, and again there was a premium on space at Willesden Lane. Unlike the children of 1939, these children had gaunt eyes that had seen things not even an adult could bear.

Mrs Cohen had decided to stay on. She had found a calling in the difficult but rewarding job of matron.

The older children were moving out to make room for younger children, and Lisa was among them. She was now 21 years old, and although it was hard for her to grasp, she had been in England for six years – many of them in this room she was now leaving.

It had been decided that Lisa would move to Mrs Canfield's. Her son had been killed by a mortar shell while dressing a soldier's wounds, and the matron had asked if Lisa would go and live with the grieving Quaker woman. Remembering her generosity during the bombing of the hostel, Lisa was only too glad to repay the debt of kindness.

Sonia, now 18, would take over Lisa's bunk. Her sister wouldn't be under the same roof, but she would be right around the corner. She helped Lisa finish cleaning out her drawers, folding her dozens of scarves, and placing her costume jewellery in a velvet bag.

Then, saving them for last, Lisa took her most prized possessions, the photos of her mother and father, and her grandmother's silver bag, and laid them reverently on top of her clothes, shutting the lid on the large suitcase and on a long chapter of her life.

Lisa left 243 Willesden Lane with her two suitcases and walked slowly down the road to Mrs Canfield's. The woman in black embraced her warmly when she arrived on the doorstep.

'This house has been quiet for too long. It has missed thee.'

As she had done years before, Lisa unpacked her things in the son's room. His on the dresser now had a black ribbon tied around it.

One week after Lisa's departure, Mrs Cohen received a call that brightened her spirits immensely. In the midst of the sea of disaster engulfing the community came a ripple of good news that she knew would be a tidal wave for two of her 'dear ones.'

She hung up the phone, ran out the door, and went bustling down the block. She was out of breath when she made it to Riffel Road.

'Lisa, Lisa! You must call Mr Hardesty at once!'

'What? What is it?' Lisa cried.

'You must call Mr Hardesty at once,' she repeated, picking up Mrs Canfield's telephone and dialling for her.

Five long days later, Lisa and Sonia were picked up by Mr Hardesty's waiting car and taken to Liverpool Street station to meet the 2:22pm train.

Lisa and Sonia waited an eternity for the train to stop. When the doors opened, a group of weary refugees appeared, their faces gaunt and haggard. Lisa watched as they descended onto the platform and came toward her. She strained to see into the approaching line of ragged people in heavy old-world overcoats. She began to tremble, imagining she was seeing her ghostly neighbours from Franzensbrückenstrasse.

The more Lisa strained to see, the more she trembled, and Sonia had to put her arms around her shoulders to hold her up.

After another eternity, they saw an

outstretched hand waving in their direction and a familiar voice shouting from down the quay.

'Lisa! Lisa! Sonia! Sonia!'

Sonia pushed Lisa forward, and from inside the mass of the crowd came a thin, handsome woman, running as fast as she could. It was Rosie. It was Rosie at last. The three sisters flew into an embrace.

They called out one another's names, 'Rosie, Sonia, Lisa!' over and over again.

When Lisa could finally pry her eyes off her sister, she looked up at Leo, who was waiting patiently for his turn to embrace them. She grabbed him around the waist and almost tripped on a beautiful four-year-old looking up at her in wonder.

Lisa gasped.

'This is our little Esther,' Rosie announced. 'Isn't she beautiful?' Then, turning to the little girl, said: 'Esther, these are your aunties, Lisa and Sonia.'

Lisa's eyes were so filled with tears she could barely see. Sonia knelt down and gave the little girl a kiss.

They went to the same restaurant in the station where Lisa had been taken with Sonia so long ago. The intervening years of war had removed the white tablecloths, and the elegant teapots had long ago been melted down for airplane parts. It was now a dingy cafeteria, but no one seemed to mind.

Leo was anxious to tell the sisters how he and Rosie had survived the last few years. Out spilled the story of their escape from Vienna as drunken tourists, the trip to freedom in Paris, then Paris falling to Hitler, then running, and running some more.

'We were always running!' Rosie explained.

'Except when we were rounded up in a holding camp outside of Lyon,' Leo interjected.

'Leo always found a way to escape,' Rosie said proudly. 'It wasn't just me, there were many people who hid us. Until I had the baby.'

Lisa and Sonia were looking with such love and admiration at their older sister that they were speechless.

'Then what happened?' Lisa begged.

'When Rosie was nine months pregnant, no one would take us in anymore, so she had to deliver the baby on the streets of Marseilles. Then we kept running until we made it to the Swiss border.'

'Leo had to lift me over the barbed wire,' Rosie broke in. 'There were Nazis shooting at us from the French side. Just after he threw Esther to one of the Swiss guards, he got shot.'

'Just in the leg,' Leo said. Sonia started to cry.

'We never gave up hope that we would see you again,' Rosie whispered.

Then the tables were turned – Rosie and Leo begged to hear all about Lisa's and Sonia's lives since their separation. When Lisa told of her scholarship, Rosie took her daughter's hand and told her, 'Your Aunt Lisa is a wonderful pianist – just like your grandmother ...'

Finally, Lisa had to ask the question they had all been waiting to ask from the moment her sister stepped off the train.

'Rosie ... do you have any news of Mama and Papa?'

Rosie looked at her sister with tears in her eyes.

'None of our letters were answered ... I have heard nothing,' she answered, then sadly pleading:

'So then, you have heard nothing also?'

'Nothing,' Lisa said. 'We have heard nothing.'

They could not bear to discuss it further, it was too hard. Rosie looked at her two younger sisters. 'Mama would be so proud of you two,' she said softly. 'And, Lisa, you know what your music meant to her … to all of us … look!'

Rosie leaned over and parted the buttons of Esther's coat. Around the little girl's neck was the chain that held the tiny gold charm of a piano.

'You have it?' Lisa cried, surprised.

Sonia spoke up. 'I gave it to Rosie when I left on the train, just like you gave it to me …'

Rosie put her arm around Sonia and said to Lisa, 'And I never took it off, until I gave it to Esther.'

Overwhelmed with the emotion of seeing the tiny charm around the neck of her new niece, Lisa felt the wall she had built up around her music beginning to give way. The forgotten promise she had made to her mother echoed in her heart.

She returned to her practising with a fervour that surprised even Mrs Floyd. She

practised every day from the moment she awoke
until the Royal Academy closed its doors at night,
throwing all her energy and passion into her
preparation. For how would the next generation
know of the music, the music Malka so loved,
if Lisa didn't honour her promise?

Chapter 26

Lisa sat nervously at the mirror in the dressing room at Wigmore Hall and tried to sit still as her sister applied a brown stripe above her eyelashes.

'Ooh, perfect! You look just like Rita Hayworth!' said Rosie, putting on the last dab. Rosie then checked her own make-up in the mirror. Life and colour had returned to her older sister's face; she looked as sophisticated as Lisa remembered.

But it was Lisa who shimmered in her red gown as she stood up and straightened the dark seams of her silk stockings and tried to calm her wildly beating heart.

Sonia ran into the dressing room from the stage, where she had been peeking out from the wings at the gathering crowd.

'It's almost full!' she cried excitedly.

'Don't go out there! They'll see you.'

'No, they won't!'

'Yes, they will!' Lisa insisted.

'Relax, the two of you, you're making me nervous,' said Rosie, intervening.

The hall was filling up quickly. Rosie had invited every person she met – people on the street, the butcher on the corner. And of course, the students and faculty of the Royal Academy would also be there.

She had also insisted that Lisa invite the nice French soldier whose address she had come across in Lisa's night table. Lisa knew he would never come, she'd met him almost a year ago, but it didn't hurt to dream.

Mrs Cohen had organised an early dinner for everyone at the hostel so that they could get to the centre of London at 7pm sharp.

Lisa's mind raced as she thought about how much had changed since her childhood fantasies of playing concerts for Viennese royalty. Instead of those adolescent dreams, she tried to focus on this audience, filled with the good people of England.

Her sisters wished her well one last time,

and she was left alone. The hush was falling; the curtain was rising.

Lisa walked elegantly on to the stage and was greeted by enthusiastic applause as she sat at the nine-foot grand.

With a subtle adjustment of her posture, she brought a hush over the audience. Once all was silent, Lisa waited a few breaths until the air of expectation was almost unbearable, then took another deep breath and went inside herself. When she felt the audience disappear, she lifted her hands in a graceful arch and began.

She started with Beethoven's *Pathétique* and had the courage to start quietly, as her mother had often counselled. She began her story with the pianissimo that recalled the quiet despair of the agonising separation from her family these past six years. The music deepened into thunderous chords retelling the years spent defiantly warding off the Nazi attacks. Lisa searched within herself and found the colours and shadings to express the depths of her longings and the heights of her triumphs.

As the intensity began to build, she sent her prayer across the footlights into the hearts of the people who had gathered together. The beauty of the music entered their souls, from the refugee to the barrister, from the garment worker to the RAF pilot, from the Resistance hero to the dockworker, and helped to guide them through their deepest, inexpressible emotions.

Mrs Cohen's eyes were shining as she allowed herself to remember and mourn her husband and sister, surely lost. Hans listened with a joy that surpassed that of any moment he had spent with Lisa in the cellar, the music bringing warmth to his darkness.

In the simple, dignified melody of the Chopin Nocturne in C Sharp Minor, Mrs Canfield faced the loss of her son, John, reliving the images of his infancy and childhood and hearing in the music the heroism of his service as a medic. In Mrs Canfield's mind, Lisa imbued the regal tones with her son's life story, one hand taking over from the other as she made the nostalgic notes evoke his life, lost but quietly remembered.

Gina and Günter held tightly to each other and felt the excitement of their future, their hearts rejoicing in the passion of Lisa's playing.

Mrs McRae, Mr Dimble, Mrs Floyd, Mr Hardesty, all of them in their way shared feelings they could never express in words. Lisa wove their stories through the Chopin and the Rachmaninoff, the music becoming the tale of so many in war-torn London.

She relived her own joys and tragedies, her terrible journey to London, and her passage to adulthood. She mourned her lost parents in the tragic tolling of the bells of the Rachmaninoff Prelude; then, from its majestic progression of chords, she built a hymn of gratitude – to her parents' love, to their wise devotion, and to every mother and father who had the courage to save their child by saying goodbye.

When enough tears had been shed in the audience, Lisa began the final piece, Chopin's heroic polonaise. This was Lisa's *tour de force*, and its thunderous exuberance raised the spirits of all assembled as row after row of shining eyes relived their proudest, bravest moments – their courage under the bombing, their unshakeable resolve, their ultimate victory.

After many seconds of awed silence, the

audience erupted in tumultuous applause. Lisa stood up and the applause grew louder. She looked into the audience and took bow after bow before leaving the stage and the glory of the spotlight.

The scene in the dressing room was utterly chaotic. The press of people included all the hostel children, shaking Lisa's hand one by one, ten women from the factory, Mr Hardesty and the staff of the Jewish Refugee Agency, Mrs Canfield and five Quaker brethren, and, of course, Sonia and Rosie and Leo and Esther.

Then came Mabel Floyd, towing a well-dressed impresario, who congratulated her profusely and spoke loudly to be heard above the din: 'Your professor tells me you play a wonderful Grieg Piano Concerto!'

Hans sat on a chair near Lisa and drank in the sound of the compliments, nodding his head in delight. Next to him stood Gina and Günter. When Mrs Cohen had finished escorting the younger children of the hostel through the informal receiving line, she asked them to stay back a minute while she said her own congratulations.

The matron watched the gracious young woman in the red gown thanking the well-wishers and pulled out her embroidered handkerchief. The beautiful vision was too much for her.

'When did this happen? You are no longer children!' she exclaimed.

Lisa, Gina, and Günter took her by the hand. 'But we are,' said Lisa. 'We will always be the children of Willesden Lane.'

At the stage door, behind another crush of well-wishers, stood a handsome French Resistance soldier wearing a discreet medal on the lapel of his uniform. He was waiting for the crowd to thin and was carrying a dozen red roses.

Rosie saw him first and, guessing who he must be, brought him over to her radiant sister. Lisa couldn't believe her eyes; she had tried to forget the image of this handsome soldier, it seemed so unlikely that they would ever meet again.

He put his hands over his heart, as he had before, to show how much he loved the music, then handed her the red roses with a card that read: 'With fervent admiration, Michel Golabek.'

Lisa clasped his hand and brought him into

the group of well-wishers forming a tight circle around her. Through her eyes brimming with tears, she surveyed the group that meant everything in the world to her, from Gina and Günter to Hans and Mrs Cohen; to her beautiful sisters, Sonia and Rosie, with Leo and Esther just behind; and now this handsome stranger who she instinctively felt would be part of her future.

Then, elated by the love and admiration surrounding her, she suddenly sensed an additional presence and was overwhelmed by a feeling of closeness to her mother. It was as if Malka were watching from above. Her heart filled with joy as she realised she had done it. She had fulfilled the promise she had made to her mother. She had held on to her music.

Epilogue

Aaron went to the United States, married, and became a successful businessman. Günter and Gina also immigrated to the United States, where they have lived happily together for more than 50 years. Hans remained in England, received his degree as a physical therapist, and went on to win numerous national chess championships for the blind. After closing the hostel at Willesden Lane, Mrs Cohen lived with her son until her death at age 70.

In the autumn of 1949, Lisa Jura received a visa allowing her to immigrate to America. Michel Golabek, who had become one of the most decorated Jewish officers in the French Resistance, followed soon after. They were married in New York in November 1949. They moved to Los Angeles, joining Rosie and Leo, who had settled there, and were followed by Sonia and her husband, Sol. The sisters remained in daily contact the rest of their lives.

In 1958, Lisa Jura was contacted by a long-lost cousin living in Israel, who wrote to her with the truth of what happened to Malka and Abraham. The cousin had received Abraham's last known communication, a letter that had been written in January 1942, and had been rerouted around the world to Palestine.

Abraham wrote of their pending deportation and implored the cousin with the words 'We are lost ... and beg you to look after our precious children.'

On 14 April 1942, they were arrested by the Gestapo, taken from their home on Franzenbrückenstrasse, and deported to Lodz. From there, they were sent to Auschwitz.

Lisa Jura had two daughters, Mona and Renee, who grew up to fulfill their mother's dream by becoming concert pianists. To this day, Mona continues to tell her mother's story on stages across the world.

Lisa's three granddaughters, Michele, Sarah and Rachel, also play the piano. Her grandson, Yoni, plays the violin.

In June 1999, Lisa's daughters and granddaughters were invited to be the featured artists at the sixtieth worldwide reunion of the Kindertransport in London. Performing the *Clair de Lune* on the BBC, Michele and Sarah thanked Britain for saving Lisa's life and spoke of the precious words given to them by their grandmother and piano teacher: 'Hold on to your music. It will be your best friend.'

It continues to be.

< Lisa and Sonia, Vienna, 1938

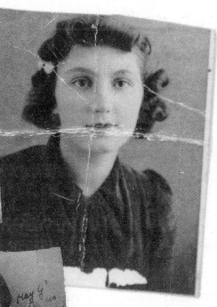

∧ Lisa, age fourteen

< Lisa Jura and
  Michel Golabek

The Children >
of Willesden
Lane, circa 1943
(in the backyard
of the hostel)